Thomas Moore, John MacHale

A Selection of Moore's Melodies

Translated Into the Irish Language by John MacHale

Thomas Moore, John MacHale

A Selection of Moore's Melodies
Translated Into the Irish Language by John MacHale

ISBN/EAN: 9783744713054

Printed in Europe, USA, Canada, Australia, Japan

Cover: Foto ©Thomas Meinert / pixelio.de

More available books at **www.hansebooks.com**

A SELECTION

OF

MOORE'S MELODIES,

Translated into the Irish Language

BY

THE MOST REVEREND JOHN MACHALE

ARCHBISHOP OF TUAM.

DUBLIN:
JAMES DUFFY, 15 WELLINGTON QUAY,
AND 22 PATERNOSTER ROW, LONDON.

1871.

PREFACE TO THE NEW EDITION

OF

MOORE'S MELODIES IN ENGLISH AND IRISH, ACCOMPANIED WITH COPIES OF THE LETTERS HE WROTE TO THE ARCHBISHOP ON THE SUBJECT OF HIS IRISH TRANSLATION.

Having published at intervals several of Moore's melodies translated into Irish, I now give an edition of them, accompanied for the most part by the original English in juxtaposition. This is an advantage of which the want has been much felt in the preceding editions. Aware of the more extensive circulation which an edition in both languages could not fail to command, I sought from the firm of Longman in London a relaxation of their copyright of the English in favor of a project which I considered would not injuriously interfere with their commercial interests. In this expectation, however, I was disappointed, although Moore himself had the kindness to interfere, as may be seen by the annexed correspondence on the subject of the Irish Melodies, now after several years published for the first time.

Time, however, the great arbiter of comflicting interests more important than those literary publications, has at length settled the question, and, by the expiration of the exclusive copyright, has released the earlier and almost the entire of those national productions. The present issue contains above eighty of those inimitable songs, comprising all of the ten numbers, which, for their national tone I deemed most deserving of an Irish translation. Of the later numbers, there are a few as yet without the English accompaniment. But, during the few unexpired years of their copyright, the reader can easily supply the blanks from the many cheap editions of the Melodies now in circulation.

Sloperton, December 10th, 1841.

MY DEAR LORD,

On my return, but a few days since, to Sloperton, I found a heap of letters awaiting me, many of which being "de omnibus rebus et quibusdam aliis", I thought might safely be left a few days without answers, and among these (from my not immediately making out the signature) was unfortunately your Lordship's. By the greatest good luck I happened, but a few minutes since, to open this packet, and lose not a moment in acquainting you with the cause of a delay which must have appeared to you so uncourteous and so unaccountable. As the post hour presses upon me, I have time at this moment for no more than to thank you most cordially for your kind and flattering communication, and to subscribe myself

Your Lordship's obliged servant,
THOMAS MOORE.

To His Grace the Most Rev. John MacHale,
Archbishop of Tuam, Tuam, Ireland.

Bowood, December, 1841.

MY DEAR LORD,

I trust that ere this you have received my letter accounting for the long delay of my answer to your very gratifying announcement. That these songs of mine should be translated into what I may call their native language, is in itself a great gratification and triumph to me; but, that such a tribute should come from the pen of your Grace, considerably adds to the pride and pleasure I feel in it.

I need hardly say that any assistance I can lend by making inquiries of publishers, or otherwise facilitating your task, shall be most heartily at your Grace's command.

I am most truly your Grace's
Faithful servant,
THOMAS MOORE.

To His Grace the Most Rev. John MacHale,
Arbhbishop of Tuam, Tuam, Ireland.

Bowood, January, 1842.

MY DEAR LORD,

Almost ever since I received your last letter, I have been in expectation of being called to town for the purpose of pursuing my labours at the State Paper Office, which will now be a long and frequent task of mine, as I have re-embarked, after a long interruption, in my Irish History. It was my intention, had I gone to town, to make such inquiries on the subject of your translation, as would be more satisfactory than any I can procure through the medium of letters. I know nothing of the state of the *property* of the work in Dublin, but in London it is in the hands of the widow of the late James Power, from whom the Longmans derive the power of publishing it. To her, therefore, any application must be made to authorize the use of either the words or the music for publication in England. I should be most sorry, I assure you, if by any of those difficulties my work were to lose the high honour you intended it by giving your translation to the world.

The letter in the newspaper which you were so kind as to send me, did not want any additional interest to its own power of language and thought; but, if it did, the sight of my own poetry (in what might be almost called its natural language) enshrined thus in the midst of *your* prose, would most abundantly afford it.

I am, my dear Lord,
Your Grace's very faithful servant,
THOMAS MOORE.

To the Most Rev. John MacHale, Archbishop of Tuam,
Tuam, Ireland.

Sloperton, April 30th, 1842.

MY DEAR LORD,

I feel really ashamed of myself for having so long delayed my acknowledgment of your great kindness; but, in addition to the usual pressure of business, I have been, lately, much and painfully occupied by the state of health in which my younger boy has returned from India. He is now, thank God, doing better, but we are still not free from alarm about him.

Your Irish (truly Irish) Melodies are a shame and a reproach to me, and I would willingly give up much of what I know of other languages to have been Irishman enough to accomplish such a work.

Yours, in great haste, but
Most truly,
THOMAS MOORE.

To His Grace the Most Rev. Doctor MacHale,
Archbishop of Tuam, Tuam, Ireland.

December 26th, 1845.

MY DEAR LORD,

I was for two reasons pleased and proud to hear from you. In the first place, to find myself kindly remembered by you, could not be otherwise than a pride and a pleasure to me, and in the next, the sight of another number of *the* Melodies relieved me from a fear which I was beginning to give way to, that you had not met with sufficient sympathy in your national work to induce you to continue it. This would, indeed, have been a pity and a shame, and I hail your new number as a proof that I was mistaken.

I find you have been able to make the metre of the Irish words exactly suit the airs, which must have been no easy achievement. I have a Latin translation of the Melodies, but of course no such *tour de force* is attempted in it.

Believe me, your Lordship's very sincere
And obliged servant,
THOMAS MOORE.

To the Most Rev. Doctor MacHale, Archbishop of Tuam,
Tuam, Ireland.

PREFACE TO THE EARLIER EDITIONS

Of the Irish Translation of Moore's Melodies.

The powerful influence of music and poetry on the feelings and habits of every people, is too well attested by experience to require an elaborate illustration. Of our incontrovertible claims to a refined and cultivated music, and to the high intellectual tone of which it is at once the index and the offspring, the few following specimens from the now classical melodies of our country furnish abundant evidence. If further proofs were wanting, they may be found in the published *Minstrelsy* of Mr. Hardiman, or the many popular songs in the possession of Mr. Bunting, to whom every Irishman owes lasting obligations for the patriotic devotion with which they have successfully laboured to rescue from oblivion some of the most valuable relics of our ancient poetry and music. That the specimens of poetry that are left us did not always correspond with the beauty of the melody that breathes through them, cannot surprise any reader familiar with the records of that ruthless spirit which, equally jealous of both, strove to involve them in the same common destruction. Against the growth and perfection of our poetry and literature, it was, alas! as they were placed within its reach, but too successful, and hence they were so impaired by repeated aggression as to be almost extinguished: whilst our music, like the morning bird, so emblematic of its sweetness and its freedom, sought safety in higher regions from the shafts of its pursuers; and whether it lighted on the valleys, or poured its wild melodies along the summits of our mountains, it always possessed the magic power of charming the wounds which were inflicted by the persecutions of the stranger.

Yet it is not from the poetical compositions of our native bards that our melodies sustained most injury. Though the dress in which they clothed their thoughts was simple, it was in general natural and graceful, and in our popular songs in the native dialect, passages might be pointed out to the classic reader not unworthy of lyrical poets of higher fame, so faithfully was the spirit of the ancient muse transmitted through the Irish Language. It was only when our music was forcibly united with the coarse and barbarous pedantry of ignorant English songsters, that it suffered from the connection. Under this yoke it continued to sink, and would probably have sunk still more, until taste should have at last shrunk from the contact of its acquaintance, had not a fond and master spirit seasonably interposed to save it from the degrading association. To MOORE our native music shall ever be indebted for clothing it in a manner befitting its dignity and lineage, and throwing over it much of the rich oriental drapery with which a congenial fancy had so amply furnished him. Thus attired, our melodies have been introduced into the most fashionable musical saloons of Europe, nay sometimes adorned in a foreign costume; but no sooner do they breathe and speak than they are at once revealed—the genuine daughters of the Land not less famed for song, than for the fidelity, heroism, and sanctity of its children. To introduce those Melodies to my humbler countrymen, robed in a manner worthy of their high origin, has been my object in the following translation. The banishing of those gross compositions with which our musical airs were oftentimes defiled will be doing a service to the taste and morality of the people: how much more so, when for them will be substituted those pure and lofty sentiments of patriotism and virtue, which those selections of the Irish Melodies so abundantly supply. The genius of Moore must ever command admiration. Its devotion to the vindication of the ancient faith of Ireland and the character of its injured people, must inspire every Irishman with still more estimable feelings. Seated amidst the tuneful followers of Apollo, he essayed the instrument of every muse, and became master of them all; sighing at length for some higher and holier source of poetical feeling, he turns to the East, and listens with rapture to its prophetic melodies; subdued by the strain, he lets fall the lyre, seizes the harp of Sion and of Erin, at once the emblem of piety and patriotism, and gives its boldest and most solemn chords to his own impassioned inspirations of country and of religion.

meaḋruiġiḋ caiṫreim ḃriain, le'r ġnaṫaċ buaiḋ.

Fonn—Maire Nic Alpin.

I.

Meaḃruiġiḋ caiṫréim Ḃriain, le'r ġnáṫaċ buaiḋ,
  Giḋ tá laċte an ġaisgiḋiġ 'na luiḋe,
Giḋ caillte do'n Ṁúmain é agus sínte 'san uaiṁ,
  'S naċ ḃ-fillfiḋ go Cion-ċorraiḋ a ċoiḋ':
An peulc úd na faiċ' fear solus naċ raiḃ fann
  Air a g-caṫ, tá anois baiṫte fa ċeó;
Aċt tá leór-ruim d'a lóċran aig lasaḋ air gaċ lann,
  Le n-ar d-treórúġaḋ ċum treise ann gaċ gleó

II.

A Ṁúmain, 'nuair do ḃronaḋ ort le féile neaṁ-ġann
  Gaċ máise, gaċ áille 'gus gaċ seun,
Ar faoileaḋ go ḃ-fuiġfiḋe air sliaḃ no a' n-gleann
  Lorg fuaċṁar oirc foirneartṁair ḋein:—
Ḃiḋeaḋ aig an Loċlanaċ seanas cinte, fíor,
  Go d-troidfeamuid sa ṡaoirse go treun,
'S gur fearr a ḃeiṫ bliaḋanta faoi ċreaċda, le ḃeiṫ saor,
  'Ná táṁ uairé a slaḃraiḋiḃ faoi leun.

III.

Na dearmadaiḋ na có-laoċra dílse, ṫug toil
  Ḃeiṫ sasṫuiġṫe go calmaċ 'sa n-gleó;
Giḋ ḃiḋ caonaċ an ġleanna dearg lé n-a ḃ-fuil,
  Níor ṫeiṫeadar, aċt ṫuiteadar d' eis clóṫ.
An ġrian, a tá d'ar soilsiúġaḋ, do ċonairc iad 'na luiḋe
  Air ḃáinseaċaiḃ Osruiḋe fá lár,
Ná ḃiḋeaḋ smúid air, ná briat-ḃróin anoċt aig dul faoi
  Fá gur ṫuiteadar gan cúitiúġaḋ san ár.

REMEMBER THE GLORIES OF BRIAN THE BRAVE.

AIR—*Molly Macalpin*

I.

Remember the glories of Brian the brave,
  Tho' the days of the hero are o'er;
Tho' lost to Mononia, and cold in the grave,
  He returns to Kinkora no more.
That star of the field, which so often hath pour'd
  Its beam on the battle, is set;
But enough of its glory remains on each sword
  To light us to victory yet.

II.

Mononia! when Nature embellish'd the tint
  Of thy fields, and thy mountains so fair,
Did she ever intend that a tyrant should print
  The footstep of slavery there?
No! Freedom, whose smile we shall never resign,
  Go, tell our invaders the Danes,
That 't is sweeter to bleed for an age at thy shrine,
  Than to sleep but a moment in chains.

III.

Forget not our wounded companions, who stood
  In the day of distress by our side;
While the moss of the valley grew red with their blood,
  They stirr'd not, but conquer'd and died.
That sun which now blesses our arms with his light
  Saw them fall upon Ossory's plain;—
Oh! let him not blush, when he leaves us to-night,
  To find that they fell there in vain.

EIRIN TA DEORA AGUS SMIGEADA DO ṠUL.

Fonn—Eilín a Rúin.

I.

Eirinn, tá deóra 'gus smígeada do ṡúl
Mar an bóġa-uisge cumtar as measgaḋ na n-dul
Lonnraċ tré ċáise deóir,
Brónaċ lár sians' go leór,
Tá do ġruanta fá dúḃan mór
Aig éirġe gaċ lá.

II.

Eirinn, ni tiormóċar do ċiún-deóir go deó;
Eirinn, ní buan beiḋeas do lag-ġáire beo:
Go raiḃ gaċ daṫ fa réir,
An-aonḟeaċt le cur go léir,
'S aig déanaḋ mar ṫuaġ na spéir'
Bóġa síoṫċáin' gaċ tráṫ.

NA COGARAIḊ AṀAIN AINM.

Fonn—An Ċailín Donn.

I.

Ná cógaraiḋe aṁáin ainm, aċt codlaḋ sé faoi sgáṫ
'S an g-cré 'fuair 'n ar cuireaḋ é go h-uaigneaċ ann a ḃláṫ:
Agus tiuġ, tuirseaċ, trom ḃiḋeaḋ deóra ar súl,
Mar ḋrúċt na h-oiḋċe ṫuiteas as néultaiḃ na n-dúl.

II.

An drúċt úr, do ṫuiteas go ciún agus go sías,
Congḃaiġeann sé an uaiṁ, ann a g-codlann sé, síor-ġlas,
'Gus na deóra, do silteas le uaigneas na h-oiḋċe,
Cuṁdoċaiḋ siad ar g-cúṁa úr ann g-croiḋe.

ERIN! THE TEAR AND THE SMILE IN THINE EYES.

AIR—*Eilin a run.*

I.

Erin! the tear and the smile in thine eyes
Blend like the rainbow that hangs in thy skies
Shining through sorrow's stream,
Saddening through pleasure's beam,
Thy suns with doubtful gleam
Weep while they rise.

II.

Erin! thy silent tear never shall cease,
Erin! thy languid smile ne'er shall increase,
Till, like the rainbow's light,
Thy various tints unite,
And form in Heaven's sight
One arch of peace!

OH! BREATHE NOT HIS NAME.

AIR—*The Brown Maid.*

I.

Oh! breathe not his name, let it sleep in the shade,
Where cold and unhonour'd his relics are laid;
Sad, silent, and dark be the tears that we shed,
As the night-dew that falls on the grass o'er his head.

II.

But the night-dew that falls, though in silence it weeps,
Shall brighten with verdure the grave where he sleeps;
And the tear that we shed, though in secret it rolls
Shall long keep his memory green in our souls.

TRA DO'N TE TA ḊUIT TAḂ'RTA NAĊ M-BEIḊ 'ĠA LUAḊ.

Fonn—Coloaḋ an t-sionaiġ.

I.

Tra do'n té tá ḋuit taḃ'rta naċ m-béiḋ,' ġa luaḋ,
Aċt a lócta 'gur aṁġar ro ġeur
A n-guilfir, trá béiḋ siad a' duḃċan glan-ċúaḋ
An te, ḋuit-se tá sínte faoi an ḃ-feur?
Guil 's ciḋ is trom, réir do naṁaid do ċáin,
Beiḋ a n-guiste 'ga ngeaḋ le do ḋeór;
Oir is cinte, ciḋ ḋoiḃ-san ḃrúċas cionntaċ aṁáin,
Go raḃ ḋuit-se mé dilis go leor.

II

Buḋ ortsa ḃi brionglóide og' ḋil mo ḃiṫ,
'S buḋ ort m' eágna aig meoṁaraḋ go síor;
'S an orċa, as deireanaiġe, racfaḋ súas ó mo ċroiḋe.
Béiḋ ar n' ainme 'g-córoinn go síor.
O 's aoiḃin do'n ċáirde, fanas beo air a t-saoġal,
Feicsin lacte do ġlóir' is mór ċáil.
Na ḋéiġ sin ni'l beannaċt ċo gar dó, a n-gaol,
Le bás air son d' áiru féin' o 'fáġail.

AN ĊRUIT, DO SCAP ṪRI ṪALLAIḊ 'N RIĠ.

Fonn—Maire a stóir.

I

An ċruit, do scap ṫrí ṫallaiḋ 'n riġ
Na gaeṫe ceólta binn',
Ta 'n ballaiḋ Teaṁra 'nois 'nn a luiḋe
Gan seársad ceoil, no ruinn:
Mar súd tá 'n t-am, ċuaiḋ ṫart, faoi ċeo,
Ta 'ċáil, 's a ċliú faoi suan;
Is croiḋṫe 'santuiġ molta teó,
Ni airiġeann iad go buan.

WHEN HE WHO ADORES THEE.

Air—*The Fox's Sleep.*

I.

When he who adores thee has left but the name
  Of his faults and his sorrows behind,
Oh! say wilt thou weep, when they darken the fame
  Of a life that for thee was resign'd?
Yes, weep, and however thy foes may condemn,
  Thy tears shall efface their decree;
For Heaven can witness, though guilty to them,
  I have been but too faithful to thee.

II.

With thee were the dreams of my earliest love;
  Every thought of my reason was thine;
In my last humble prayer to the Spirit above,
  Thy name shall be mingled with mine.
Oh! blest are the lovers and friends who shall live
  The days of thy glory to see:
But the next dearest blessing that Heaven can give
  Is the pride of thus dying for thee.

THE HARP THAT ONCE THROUGH TARA'S HALLS.

Air—*Molly Astore.*

I.

The harp that once through Tara's halls
  The soul of music shed,
Now hangs as mute on Tara's walls
  As if that soul were fled.
So sleeps the pride of former days,
  So glory's thrill is o'er,
And hearts that once beat high for praise
  Now feel that pulse no more.

II.

Ni cluinntear cruit na Teaṁra treun
  Measg cruinniúġaḋ ban no saoi,
'Oir fuasgrann, i ḃeiṫ feacṫa, faon,
  Fuaim briste teud sa n-oiḋċe.
Mar súd do'n t-saorsaċt. 's anaṁ trá
  A dúsgṫar i go deó,
Aċt 'nuair a bristear croiḋe 'g a ċráḋaḋ,
  Aig foilsiúġaḋ i ḃeiṫ beó.

NA SÍL GUR SÍOR-ARD AGUS AERAĊ MO ĊROIḊE.

Fonn—Seaġan O'Raġallaiġ Clisteaċ.

I.

Na síl gur síor-ard agus aeraċ mo ċroiḋe
No ó linduiḃ ċo saor agus ciúċear sa trá;
No go ḃ-fanaiḋ an smig lasas suarcas na h-oiḋċe
  Air mo leacaiḃ air maidin gan smuid air bíċ cráḋ
Ní'l an sa 't-saoġal so aċt fasaċ neaṁ-ċorraċ
Naċ ḃ-feicṫear aċt anaṁ an rós ann sa t-sliġe
'S an láṁ is mo santuiġ an ḃláṫ trío a g-corraċ
Si 's luaiṫe ġuinear na deilg ta faoi.
Aċt cuir ċart an ċuaċ 's air feaḋ seal' suilḃir bíḋ,
Ó ṁí-aḋ ar m-beaṫa beiḋ cuṁduiġṫe go leor
Le deor ṫig o smig' ḋealruiġear gardoċas croiḋe
  Agus smig' iompuiġear teagar na truaġa ċum deor

II.

Is cinte gur dorċa ḃeiḋeaḋ eige ar m-bíḋ
Gan e ḃeiṫ fiġte le suarcas 's le gráḋ
'Gur d'-ḟagfain mo ḃeannaċt aig a t-saoġal so a ċoiḋċe
  Nuair a ċailfaid na seoda ud 'sgeiṁ a's a m-bláṫ.
Do'n te buḋ fearr cuman, se buḋ doiġe ḃeiṫ mealṫa
Aig eugcaoin na h-aisling' do ḃreuguiġ a ċroiḋe.
S an te buḋ mó ṁuinin as muintear 's a ġealta
Is aoiḃin mar caraḋ do, feall air a ṡliġe

II

No more to chiefs and ladies bright
  The harp of Tara swells;
The chord alone, that breaks at night,
  Its tale of ruin tells.
Thus Freedom now so seldom wakes,
  The only throb she gives
Is when some heart indignant breaks,
  To show that still she lives.

OH! THINK NOT MY SPIRITS ARE ALWAYS AS LIGHT.

AIR—*John O'Reily the Active.*

I.

Oh! think not my spirits are always as light,
  And as free from a pang, as they seem to you now:
Nor expect that the heart-beaming smile of to-night
  Will return with to-morrow to brighten my brow,
No:—life is a waste of wearisome hours,
  Which seldom the rose of enjoyment adorns;
And the heart that is soonest awake to the flowers
  Is always the first to be touch'd by the thorns.
But send round the bowl, and be happy awhile:—
  May we never meet worse in our pilgrimage here,
Than the tear that enjoyment may gild with a smile,
  And the smile that compassion can turn to a tear!

II.

The thread of our life would be dark, Heaven knows!
  If it were not with friendship and love intertwined;
And I care not how soon I may sink to repose,
  When these blessings shall cease to be dear to my mind
But they who have lov'd the fondest, the purest,
  Too often have wept o'er the dream they believ'd;
And the heart that has slumber'd in friendship securest
  Is happy indeed if 't was never deceiv'd.

Aċt cuir ṫart an ċuaċ, 's ċoad 's ḟanas de ġaeṫ
Na rinne géille aig fear na aig mnaoi,
Bíḋeaḋ grian leus an ċumain air ṁadin air lae
Gur ré solais muintir da ḋealruġaḋ dul faoi.

GIḊ SO M' AṀARC DEIĠIONAĊ AIR EIRINN A CAOIḊ.

Fonn—Lin Cúlean.

I.

Giḋ so m'aṁarc déiġionaċ air Eirinn a caoiḋ,
Geabfad Eire 'nn gaċ tír, a m-béiḋiḋ cuisle mo ċroiḋe:
'Béiḋ d' ueċt mar ṫeaċ-ḋídin, a ċéile mo ċlaon,
Is do rosg mar réalt-eóluis a n-geur-ḃruid a g-cian.

II.

Go cluain uaigneaċ fásaiġ, no cuan coiṁḋeaċ, gorg,
Ann naċ féidir lé'r náṁaid ar g-coisceim do lorg,
Ealóċad lé mo ċúilḟionn, 'sní aireóċaiḋ mé an síon
Ċo geur leis an náṁaid, tá d'ar n-díbirt as díon.

III.

Dearcfad air ór-ḟolt tiuġ, fáinneaċ do ċinn,
Is éisdfead le ceólṫaiḃ do ċláirsiġe tá binn,
Gan eagla go scróicfeaḋ an Sasanaċ teann
Aon teud as do ċruit, no aon dlaoiġ as do ċeann

BUḊ LUAĊṀAR, TEARC, SEOIDE NA H-OIĠ-ṀNA SAIṀ'.

Fonn—Ta an saṁra teaċt.

I.

Buḋ lúaċṁar, tearc, seóide na h-oiġ-ṁná saiṁ'
Agus fáinne de'n ór air a b-ḟleasg ann a láiṁ.
Aċt buḋ lonnraiġe go fada a sgéiṁ is a bláṫ
'Ná an ór-ḟlat 'sna seúide, d'a áille 's d' a ḃreáġa.

But send round the bowl: while a relic of truth
  Is in man or in woman, this prayer shall be mine—
That the sunshine of love may illumine our youth,
  And the moonlight of friendship console our decline.

THOUGH THE LAST GLIMPSE OF ERIN.

AIR—*Coulin.*

I.

Tho' the last glimpse of Erin with sorrow I see,
Yet wherever thou art shall seem Erin to me;
In exile thy bosom shall still be my home,
And thine eyes make my climate wherever we roam.

II.

To the gloom of some desert or cold rocky shore,
Where the eye of the stranger can haunt us no more,
I will fly with my Coulin, and think the rough winds
Less rude than the foes we leave frowning behind.

III.

And I 'll gaze on thy gold hair, as graceful it wreathes,
And hang o'er thy soft harp, as wildly it breathes;
Nor dread that the cold-hearted Saxon will tear
One chord from that harp, or one lock from that hair.

RICH AND RARE WERE THE GEMS SHE WORE.

AIR—*The summer is coming.*

I.

Rich and rare were the gems she wore,
And a bright gold ring on her wand she bore;
But ah! her beauty was far beyond
Her sparkling gems or snow-white wand.

II.

Nać iongnaḋ do'n ṁaiġdean, a d' ḟiafruiġ an saoi,
Ḃeiṫ siúḃal go h-aonarać a n-uaigneas na sliġe,
Ḃ-fuil subáilciḋe óig-fear na h-Eireann ċo mór,
'S nać d-tnuṫfaḋ go truaillíḋ lé ainnḟir no ór?

III.

Do ḟreagair, níl eagla nó buaiḋirt air mo ċroiḋe,
Ni ḋéanfaiḋ clann Eireann dam doċar no díṫ;
Giḋ claónṁar air ḋeire iad 's air ṡeóidiḃ go leór,
Is annsa leó coinġioll a's cáiḋe go mór.

IV.

Lé smíġeaḋ sgíaṁaċ, lasta ó ionracas croiḋe,
Ṡiúḃal an óig-ḃean go muiníġneaċ iomlán na críċ',
Is beannaċt do'n té, aig a raiḃ dóṫċus as cáil
Na b-flaṫa saoi-ḃeusaċ, feara fíor Innse-fáil.

MAR ĠAṪ SOILSEAĊ GREINE AIR LINN DUḂ 'NA LUIḊE

Fonn—Aislin an óig fir.

I.

Mar ġaṫ soilseaċ gréine air linn duḃ 'na luiḋe
Is fuar-ṫuil' na b-fóirsi lé fánaḋ dul faoi,
Ḃíḋeas an leaca ḃíḋeas lasta le smigeḋ sgiaṁaċ, bláḋ,
'S an croiḋe stiġ lé trom-ualaċ dubróin d'á ċráḋaḋ.

II.

Aon ċuiṁne aṁáin cuṁaṁail gan táṁ, ḃíḋeas síor-ḃeó,
'S aig silt air ar Laċṫiḃ a ḋúḃain 's a ċeó,
Nać d-tigeann air, áṫrúġaḋ ó lannair, nó neul,
S' a ṁáoluġaḋ nó a ḃuaiḋreaḋ go sáróċaḋ an saoġal.

III.

Béiḋ an ċuiṁne úd d'ar n-gonaḋ lár sleiḋe gan sgíṫ,
Mar ḋuilleóg ċríon saṁraiḋ air ċraoḃ crainn 'na luiḋe,
A gealtar le gaċṫiḃ na gréine air a n-geug,
'S nać n-úraiġeann na ḋiaiḋ sin, lé n'a ṫéagar go h-eug.

II.

"Lady! dost thou not fear to stray,
"So lone and lovely, through this bleak way?
"Are Erin's sons so good or so cold
"As not to be tempted by woman or gold?"

III.

"Sir Knight! I feel not the least alarm;
"No son of Erin will offer me harm:—
"For though they love woman and golden store,
"Sir Knight! they love honour and virtue more".

IV.

On she went, and her maiden smile
In safety lighted her round the green isle;
And blest for ever is she who relied
Upon Erin's honour and Erin's pride.

A BEAM O'ER THE FACE OF THE WATERS MAY GLOW.

AIR—*The young man's dream.*

I.

As a beam o'er the face of the waters may glow,
While the tide runs in darkness and coldness below,
So the cheek may be ting'd with a warm sunny smile,
Though the cold heart to ruin runs darkly the while.

II.

One fatal remembrance, one sorrow that throws
Its bleak shade alike o'er our joys and our woes,
To which life nothing darker or brighter can bring,
For which joy has no balm and affliction no sting:

III.

Oh! this thought in the midst of enjoyment will stay,
Like a dead leafless branch in the summer's bright ray;
The beams of the warm sun play round it in vain;
It may smile in his light, but it blooms not again.

NÍ Ḃ-FUIL ANSA G-CRUINNE AON ĊUMAR, NO GLEANN.

Fonn—Sean ceann Donaċa.

I.

Ní ḃ-fuil ansa g-cruinne aon ċumar, no gleann,
Mar an lag a ḃ-fuil có-sruṫ na dís' aḃann ann;
Is luaiṫe ḃéiḋeas éalaiġṫe uaim m' anmann, 's mo ḃríġ,
'Na ċríonfas an gleann glas úd úr as mo ċroiḋe.

II.

Ní hé an t-aṁarc breáġ, aoiḃinn ḃí sgarṫa air gaċ taoḃ,
Ní hé lonnair an ċriostáil, ná úr-ḃláṫ na g-craoḃ,
Ní hé coṁgar na sruṫa mar euġ-ċeól mná-síġe,
Aċt níḋ éigin níos dílse tá a n-doiṁneaċt an ċroiḋe:

III.

Siad mo ċáirde, do ċeangail mo ċumann 's mo ċlaon,
Do scap air gaċ níḋ ann, sgéiṁ ṡársa na mían;
Oir ní'l aon níḋ d'a áille naċ méaduiġeann a ḃláṫ,
D'a ḟeicsin tre ṡúiliḃ air a m-biḋeann againn gráḋ.

IV.

A ġleann aoiḃinn ċaṫ-aḃna, buḋ suaiṁneaċ mo ṡuan
Faoi ḟasgaḋ do ċáḃáin lé mo ċara fíor-ḃuan,
'N áit a m-béiḋmuid ó na síontaiḃ faoi ḋídean go sáiṁ
'S ar g-croiḋṫe mar do ċiún-ṡruṫa cóiṁeasgṫa lé dáiṁ.

NAOṀ SENÁN AGUS AN ḂEAN-ĊUARTA.

Fonn— An draḋanán donn.

I

O! deifriġ a's fág, an long gan áḋ,
An inis ḃeannuiġ' roiṁ an lá;
Oir air do ḃord, giḋ is dorċaḋ an oiḋċe
Ciḋim cuma, is dual do mnaoi:
Oir se mo ṁoid' sa'n i so, cló
Cois' mna naċ ḃ-fagfar ann go deo.

THE MEETING OF THE WATERS.

Air—*The old head of Denis.*

I.

There is not in this wide world a valley so sweet
As that vale in whose bosom the bright waters meet;
Oh! the last ray of feeling and life must depart,
Ere the bloom of that valley shall fade from my heart.

II.

Yet it *was* not that Nature had shed o'er the scene
Her purest of crystal and brightest of green;
'T was not the soft magic of streamlet or rill,
Oh! no—it was something more exquisite still.

III.

'T was that friends, the belov'd of my bosom, were near,
Who made every dear scene of enchantment more dear,
And who felt how the best charms of nature improve,
When we see them reflected from looks that we love.

IV.

Sweet Vale of Avoca! how calm could I rest
In thy bosom of shade, with the friends I love best,
Where the storms that we feel in this cold world should cease,
And our hearts, like thy waters, be mingled in peace.

ST. SENANUS AND THE LADY.

I.

"Oh! haste and leave this sacred isle,
"Unholy bark, ere morning smile;
"For on thy deck, though dark it be,
"A female form I see;
"And I have sworn this sainted sod
"Shall ne'er by woman's foot be trod".

II.

O aṫair! na cuir ṫríd an t-sruṫ,
Mo ḃád lán fíonta 's tonnta duḃ';
Toirnġim ḃeiṫ go h-uṁal ó ċroiḋe
Roimt d' orṫa maiḋne a's oiḋċe,
Ḟir ḃeannuiġṫe ni 'l aon áḋḃar sgaṫ'
Go milfaḋ mo ċos an t-úr no ḃláṫ.

III.

Níor ḋconnuiġ áird do ġuṫ na mna
'Gur d' ḟill an long le cóir 'sa trá,
Aċt da n-déanfaḋ an óig-ḃean sgiṫ
Ann go d-ti críoċ na h oiḋċe,
Do réir na sgeulṫ' buḋ ṁór an baoġal
Naċ d-treigfaḋ an t-oileán le n-a saoġal.

naċ aoiḃin uair aig tomaḋ gréiné anns an ḃ-fraiġ.

Fonn—Casaḋ an t-súgain.

I.

Naċ aoiḃin uair aig tomaḋ gréine anns a' ḃ-fráiġ,
'S a solus sínte air a g-ciún-tonn go tráiġ!
Tig ó aimsir arsa, aisling tiúġ leis an n-oiḋċe,
Aig dúsaċt cúṁa ar g-cairde, úr ann ar g-croiḋe.

II.

Trá ḋearcaim Lóċrann lag an lae aig dul faoi,
'S an áiḋḃéis daiṫte leis an or-sgáil buiḋe;
Triḋ ṫonna lonnraċ' tnuṫaim, triall siar go cuan
Na h-innse áille, a ḃ-fuiġead ann feun 'gur suan.

II.

"O Father! send not hence my bark,
"Through wintry winds and o'er billows dark.
"I come with humble heart to share
"Thy morn and evening prayer:
"Nor mine the feet, O holy Saint,
"The brightness of thy sod to taint".

III.

The Lady's prayer Senanus spurn'd;
The winds blew fresh, the bark return'd:
But legends hint, that had the maid
Till morning's light delay'd,
And given the saint one rosy smile,
She ne'er had left his lonely isle.

HOW DEAR TO ME THE HOUR.

AIR—*The twisting of the rope.*

I.

How dear to me the hour when daylight dies,
And sunbeams melt along the silent sea,
For then sweet dreams of other days arise,
And memory breathes her every sigh to thee.

II.

And, as I watch the line of light, that plays
Along the smooth wave tow'rd the burning west,
I long to tread that path of golden rays,
And think 't will lead to some bright isle of rest.

Dileaḋ an ḟiliḋ.

Fonn—Air seaċrán.

I.

Trá ciún n'eis ḃáis ḃeiḋeas sínte claon,
Beir ċum mo ċeile ġraḋaiġe, mo ċroiḋe:
Di innis gur ċoṫuiġ é smuig' a's sgaiṫ fíon',
Có'ad a's air an t-saoġal so, 'nna coṁnuiḋe bí,
Léi, abair gan silt aon deor aṁáin gola
A líonfaḋ le lionn-duḃ brón a croiḋe,
Aċt braon a ṫairgeaḋ de ċaor fíon fola
Cum an fuiġioll a ḃeiṫ falcṫa gaċ lá a's oiḋċe.

II.

'Nuair ḃeiḋeas solus mo ċeol' 'nna luiḋe
Béir mo ċláirseaċ go d-tí do lann,
Croċ í suas le h-ais dorus an tiġe
'Ḃ-faġann súḃalaiḋ' tuirseaċ' sgiṫ fáilteaṁail ann;
'S trá déanfas bard boċt seaċrain' searaḋ'
A duraċt a teuda as suan go rinn,
Bíḋeaḋ cuiṁne air an ḃ-file air leis í, a lasaḋ,
Do smiġ do leanḃ na g-ceolta binn.

III.

Conḃuiġ, a's é 'nois faoi ṁaol, an sgála
Ċum, -n'éis me imṫeaċt,—ḃeiṫ air do ċlár
Aċt beul gan cuman aig sléiḋ no dala
Go deo ni ḃlaisfiḋ deor as a ḃárr.
Aċt ma ḃiḋeann fear fíor gan claon i ṁeallaḋ,
As ólfas d' a rún naċ dual a ċráḋ,
Mo ġaeṫe beiḋ 'g eitioll teaċt ann réir ġeallaḋ,
'Gur beannuġaḋ gaċ braon de 'n g-cuaċ 'sa trá.

THE BARD'S LEGACY.

AIR—*Wanting.*

I.

When in death I shall calm recline,
Oh! bear my heart to my mistress dear:
Tell her it liv'd upon smiles and wine
Of the brightest hue, while it linger'd here.
Bid her not shed one tear of sorrow,
To sully a heart so brilliant and light;
But balmy drops of the red grape borrow,
To bathe the relic from morn till night.

II.

When the light of my song is o'er,
Then take my harp to your ancient hall;
Hang it up at that friendly door,
Where weary travellers love to call.
Then if some bard, who roams forsaken,
Revive its soft notes in passing along,
Oh! then let one thought of its master waken
Your warmest smiles for the child of song.

III.

Keep this cup, which is now o'erflowing,
To grace your revel when I 'm at rest;
Never, oh! never its balm bestowing
On lips that beauty hath seldom blest.
But when some warm devoted lover
To her he adores shall bathe its brim,
Then, then my spirit around shall hover,
And hallow each drop that foams for him.

NAC MINIC DO ĠUIL AN BEAN-SIĠE.

Fonn—An oig-bean dub ionṁuin.

I.

Naċ minic do ġuil an bean-síġe!
Naċ minic do ċráiḋ bás an croiḋe,
Aig sgaolaḋ gaċ cuing 'sa trá,
Do ḋealb glóir, no graḋ.
Do gaċ aon laoċ calma tá sínte
Suan! 's do ġaċ súil tá neulṁar le caointe!
Air a n-uaiṁ, ann a g-coḋlann an luan,
Guileaḋ na h-óiġe 's na gairgiḋiġ go buan.

II.

Is dub an t-am ann a b-fuilmuid beó,
Soluis d'eis a ċéile faoi ċeó;
'S gaċ aon, a sear lóċrann mar reul
Triḋ Eire, anois múċta faoi neull.
'S trom deor an té, b-fuil a ċroiḋe 'g a ḃriseaḋ,
Ḃ-fuil eugṫa a ṡó, 's a ḋóiġ 'ga ċliseaḋ:
Aċt aig aise an ḟlaṫa is geal go leór,
Do ṫuitear air a ċróċar an deór.

III.

Tá ar leus-ṁara múċta gan daṫ,
Tu-sa, a Ċoin na g-ceud caṫ!
'S tú eile! 's air do ḃriaṫraib teó
Ḃí suan, saoirse a's fírinn, beó—
Dís eugṫa,—fad beiḋear gairgiḋeaċt lannraċ,
No daoineaċt sa ġeur-ċreaċ cogaiḋ sgannraċ,
Béiḋ a m-beaṫa 's a m-bás ann gaċ dáil
'Ga g-canaḋ trí úr Innis-fáil.

HOW OFT HAS THE BENSHEE CRIED.

AIR—*The dear black maid.*

I.

How oft has the Benshee cried,
How oft has death untied
Bright links that Glory wove,
Sweet bonds entwin'd by Love!
Peace to each manly soul that sleepeth;
Rest to each faithful eye that weepeth;
Long may the fair and brave
Sigh o'er the hero's grave!

II.

We 're fall'n upon gloomy days!
Star after star decays,
Every bright name that shed
Light o'er the land is fled.
Dark falls the tear of him who mourneth
Lost joy, or hope that ne'er returneth:
But brightly flows the tear
Wept o'er a hero's bier.

III.

Quench'd are our beacon lights—
Thou, of the Hundred Fights!
Thou, on whose burning tongue
Truth, peace, and freedom hung!
Both mute—but long as valour shineth,
Or mercy's soul at war repineth,
So long shall Erin's pride
Tell how they lived and died.

SUD AIR SIUBAL ṪRÍD AN G-CRUINNE.

Fonn—Garrḋá Eoin.

I.

Súd air siuḃal ṫríd an g-cruinne mar leimḃ láir fleiḋ',
Táḃairt blas' de rud milis, a's de rud eile' mian
'S nuair a ċuirsiġeas an sians 'sa g-cruċ soir ḃíḋeas teiṫ,
Ċum tír 'siar ḃeiṫ 'triallaḋ bíḋeann againn claon.
Má's measg na seoide is áille, is gnaṫaċ',
Truaġ-ċroiḋṫe aireaṁ, 'gus roisg gan ceo,
Ni éigin duinn imṫeaċt as ar d-tír féin gráḋaċ
'Cur tóir' air rún searcaṁail 'gus súile beo,
'Nois cuiṁniġ, aig dul ṫart do'n sgála ar a' g-clár
Ma's soirṁar, no siarṁur ḃeiḋeas d' aisdir sa t-sliġe
Trá ċum sláinte mna, 'ḃeiḋeas cuaċ líonta go bár
Na dearmuid an smig lasas fasgaḋ do ṫiġe.

II.

A g-cruċ Sacsan bíḋeann garrḋa na deise, faoi sgáṫ,
Aig naṫair leacantaċ, 'g a ḟaire mar ṁaor;
Aċt ċo trom ḃíḋeas 'nna codlaḋ an naṫair gaċ trá,
Go b-fagṫar an ġairdín gan faire ma 's fíor.
Ní'l ann, fál milseaċ dorsaṁail geur,
Mar bíḋeas ann Eirinn ' coimirc a bláṫ
A ṫéiġeas ar g-ceudfaiḋ trá ġoineas ar meur'
Taḃairt teagair do'n ċroiḋe tra ḃíḋeas 'ga ċráḋ.
'Nois cuiṁniġ, (mar ta ṡuas).

III.

'Sa b-Frainc 'nuair sgaoileas bean-ċeile ċum sráiġ'
Síor-ḃuarṫa an ṗórta, a seolta lán',
Is anaṁ gníḋeas graḋ aċt a treoruġaḋ o'n tráiġ
'g a fágail, aig impiḋe di "aisdir slán".

WE MAY ROAM THRO' THIS WORLD.

I.

We may roam thro' this world, like a child at a feast,
  Who but sips of a sweet, and then flies to the rest;
And, when pleasure begins to grow dull in the east,
  We may order our wings, and be off to the west;
But if hearts that feel, and eyes that smile,
  Are the dearest gifts that Heaven supplies,
We never need leave our own green isle,
  For sensitive hearts and for sun-bright eyes.
Then remember, wherever your goblet is crown'd,
  Thro' this world, whether eastward or westward you roam,
When a cup to the smile of dear woman goes round,
  Oh! remember the smile that adorns her at home.

II.

In England, the garden of Beauty is kept
  By a dragon of prudery, plac'd within call;
But so oft this unamiable dragon has slept,
  That the garden 's but carelessly watch'd after all.
Oh! they want the wild sweet-briery fence
  Which round the flowers of Erin dwells;
Which warns the touch while winning the sense,
  Nor charms us least when it most repels.
Then remember, wherever your goblet is crown'd,
  Thro' this world, whether eastward or westward you roam,
When a cup to the smile of dear woman goes round,
  Oh! remember the smile that adorns her at home.

III.

In France, when the heart of a woman sets sail
  On the ocean of wedlock its fortune to try,
Love seldom goes far in a vessel so frail,
  But just pilots her off, and then bids her good-bye.

Aċt inġeana Eireann congḃuiġeann gan sgiṫ
An t-óglaċ gaḃṫa, le fonn a raṁ
Tríḋ sgalan' gréine 'gur síonta gaoṫ'
Mar ḃí 'nuair a ċuir se a long air snáṁ
'Nois cuiṁniġ (mar sé suas).

bíḋeaḋ cuiṁne aig éirinn air na laeṫiḃ do ḃí.

Fonn—An Sionnaċ ruaḋ.

I.

Bíḋeaḋ cuiṁne aig Eirinn air na laeṫiḃ, do ḃí,
Sul do ḃraiṫ 'a clann féin í le feill-ḃeart,
Nuair ḃí ioḋ de 'n ór-ḃuiḋe air ḃrágaid Maoilseaclainn an ríġ,
Do ḃuaiḋ ó'n naṁ, ḃí uailleaċ as all-neart:
'Nuair sgaoil a ríġte brat glas na Craoḃ-ruaiḋ'
Taḃairt a laoċra ċum caṫa go claonṁar,
Sul do facas seóide Eireann aig dealraḋ go nuaḋ
A g-cróin-ḟleasg an t-Sasanaiġ treunṁair.

II.

Trá ḃíḋeas air loċ Néaċaiḋ an t-iasgaire aig siúḃal
Le linn solus lae ḃeiṫ aig faonaḋ,
Cíḋeann sean-ċloigṫiġ síos, nuair ḃíḋeas go h-úṁal
Air ḃruaċ na linne aig claonaḋ:
Mar súd, tré aisling ḃíḋmuid aig fáġail
Lag-leus air na laeṫiḃ tá a g-cianta,
'S go brónaċ aig dearcaḋ air a n-glóir faoi sgáil,
Ta báiṫte faoi ṫrom-ṫona bliaḋanta.

While the daughters of Erin keep the boy,
  Ever smiling beside his faithful oar,
Through billows of woe and beams of joy,
  The same as he looked when he left the shore.
Then, remember, wherever your goblet is crown'd,
  Thro' this world, whether eastward or westward you roam,
When a cup to the smile of dear woman goes round,
  Oh! remember the smile that adorns her at home.

LET ERIN REMEMBER THE DAYS OF OLD.

AIR—*The Red Fox.*

I.

Let Erin remember the days of old,
  Ere her faithless sons betray'd her;
When Malachi wore the collar of gold,
  Which he won from her proud invader;
When her kings with standard of green unfurl'd,
  Led the Red-Branch Knights to danger;—
Ere the emerald gem of the western world
  Was set in the crown of a stranger.

II.

On Lough Neagh's bank as the fisherman strays,
  When the clear cold eve 's declining,
He sees the round towers of other days
  In the wave beneath him shining.
Thus shall memory often, in dreams sublime,
  Catch a glimpse of the days that are over;
Thus, sighing, look through the waves of time
  For the long-faded glories they cover.

BÍḊEAḊ SUAN ORT, ṠRUṪ, ṀAOILLE.

Fonn—Arreaḋ m' Eiblín ḋílis.

I.

Bíḋeaḋ suan ort, ṡruṫ, Ṁaoille, tá borrṫa le ḋíle,
Na buairḋeaḋ na síonta do ċiun-tuile lán,
Tá aig éirdeaċt 's an oiḋċe le gol inġín' Lire
Aig éagcaoin na n-gearsa d' ḟág í le fán.
Cá h-am béiḋear an ala aig foir-ċeann a draoiḋeaċta,
Cá h-am do ċluinfear a h-eug-ċeol air toinn?
Cá h-am do buailfear dam árd-ċloga riġeaċta
Na b-flaṫas, do m' ḟáiltiuġaḋ ó'n t-saoġal so go binn?

II.

Air do ṫonn ġarb ġeiṁriḋ, monuair! béiḋid mo ċaointe,
Aig fuagraḋ mo ḋraoiḋeaċta tré na saoġalta go buan,
'Na ḟad tá 'Eire faoi ċuibreaiġ' a geur-náṁaid, sínte,
Aig feiṫeaḋ air a n-uair le n-a dúsaċt ó suan:
Cá h-am éireoċas reult lonnraċ aig soilsiúġaḋ
Air sáiṁ-inis Eireann lán-lóċrann an lae?
Cá h-am do ċluinfear ceol ḟlaṫais aig soilsiuġaḋ,
Gur fáiltiġeaḋ Fionnuala go naoṁ-áras Dé?

GRIAN-ḂOṪ EIBLÍN.

Fonn—Air Seaċrán.

I.

Bí 'caoineaḋ an ama
Trá ċum Eiblín' leaṁa
Ṫainic tiarna an gleana le geallta breug',
Bí an ġeallaċ faoi neul
'Sníor las 'sa speur aon reul
Le cuṁa, gur ċaill an óg-bean a clú go h-eug.

THE SONG OF FIONNULA.

AIR—*Arrah, my dear Eveleen.*

I.

Silent, O Moyle! be the roar of thy water,
  Break not, ye breezes, her chain of repose,
While, murmuring mournfully, Lir's lonely daughter
  Tells to the night-star her tale of woes.
When shall the swan, her death-note singing,
  Sleep, with wings in darkness furl'd?
When will heaven, its sweet bells ringing,
  Call my spirit from this stormy world?

II.

Sadly, O Moyle! to thy winter wave weeping,
  Fate bids me languish long ages away;
Yet still in her darkness doth Erin lie sleeping,
  Still doth the pure light its dawning delay.
When will that day-star, mildly springing,
  Warm our isle with peace and love?
When will heaven, its sweet bell ringing,
  Call my spirit to the fields above?

EVELEEN'S BOWER.

AIR—*Wanting.*

I.

Oh! weep for the hour
When to Eveleen's bower
The Lord of the Valley with false vows came;
The moon hid her light
From the heavens that night,
And wept behind the clouds at the maiden's shame.

II.

Ní raiḃ le faġail
Air an rae caiḋe, sgáil,
'Oir ḃris amaċ arís a leus go luaṫ;
Aċt co'aḋ 's ḃeiḋear sí beo
Ní sgarfar arís go deo
An flám a ṫuit air Eiblín duḃaċan a tuaḋ.

III.

Ḃí an sneaċta' 'na luiḋe
Air ċéim ċumang na sliġe
Ṫríd an m-bogaċ ann air ḟill an Tiarna ó 'n gleann;
Agus is iomḋa lorg nuaḋ,
'Sa t-sneaċta, milleaḋ a t-snuaḋ,
D' Ḟoillsiġ a ċéim ċum an tiġe rai Eiblín ann.

IV.

Leáġ grian an lae
Le teas-ḃriġ a gae
Gaċ lorg d'ḟag feall-ċos an Tiġarna gan croiḋe,
Aċt aig gaeṫe neiṁe aṁain,
Tá glanaḋ 'maċ an ċáin
D' ḟan air 'cail 'ḃarr do-ḃeirt na h-oiḋċe.

B' ARD É AN FUAGRAḊ.

Fonn—An rógaire duḃ.

I.

B'árd é an fuagraḋ, ó 'n t-saoirse do ġáir,
Agus b' aoiḃin an uair, do ṫug Spáinniġ air fáir
  Aig dúraċt ċum dioġaltais ar geibeal oirc ċruaiḋ!
O! a ḟaoirse! ná fáġṫar air d' aigne aon sgíṫ,
Go d-téiḋir ṫar an iar-ṁuir go deifireaċ, mar ġaoṫ;
Taḃair solus do ġnúise do gaċ áit, tá 'g a ċráḋaḋ,
'S ná ceill air ġlas-ḟeamróg na h-Eireann do ġráḋ
  Aig síġeaḋ craoḃ-ola Spainneaċ air ċróm-ḟleasg do ḃuaiḋ'.

II.

The clouds pass'd soon
From the chaste cold moon,
And heaven smil'd again with her vestal flame;
But none will see the day
When the clouds shall pass away,
Which that dark hour left on Eveleen's fame.

III.

The white snow lay
On the narrow path-way,
When the Lord of the Valley cross'd over the moor;
And many a deep print
On the white snow's tint
Show'd the track of his footsteps to Eveleen's door.

IV.

The next sun's ray
Soon melted away
Every trace on the path where the false Lord came;
But there 's a light above,
Which alone can remove
That stain upon the snow of fair Eveleen's fame.

SUBLIME WAS THE WARNING.

AIR—*The Black Joke.*

I.

Sublime was the warning that Liberty spoke,
And grand was the moment when Spaniards awoke
Into life and revenge from the conqueror's chain.
O Liberty! let not this spirit have rest,
Till it move, like a breeze, o'er the waves of the west;
Give the light of your look to each sorrowing spot,
Nor, oh! be the Shamrock of Erin forgot,
While you add to your garland the Olive of Spain!

II.

Má ḃeir oiġreaċt ċeirt sinsear, a's oiġreaċt a d-tuaḋ,
Do gaċ tír a's gaċ teallaċ snás sgiaṁac a's snuaḋ,
Má's loc an feall 's má ḃeir aṁras leis cáin!
A ġaisgiḋiġ na h-Ibire, is ionann ar sliġe,
Is bíḋeaḋ se gan leac, no deor ċaointe 'nna luiḋe
Beiḋeaḋ feiṫeaḋ air ḃás air biṫ buḋ cluṫaiġe dó
'Na ḃeiṫ air uiṁir na m-buaḋaċ aig tuitim 'sa n-gleo,
Fá ṡeamróg na h-Eireann 's craoḃ-ola na Spáinn'.

III.

A ḃlácaiġ is Uí Ḋóṁnaill, 'ṫréig tír ġlas na m-beann,
Ann ar h-oileaḋ ḃur n-óige 's naċ raiḃ le fáġail ann
An dídean 's an fásgaḋ, do fuair siḃ a g-cian:
Guiḋiḋ an leus a ḃí lasta le ḃur saor-ġaoṫ, ḃeiṫ ḃeo
Ann Eirinn, go soilseaċ gan corruġaḋ, gan ceo;
'S ná tógḃaiḋe air ċríċ Sacsan ḃeiṫ go mall a's go fann
Aig tarraing sa g-comrac n-aġaiḋ náṁaid a lann
Air son craoḃ-ola Spáinneaċ a's bláṫ Eireann na ḃ-fian.

IV.

Bail Dé air an tionsgnaḋ! ní clisfiḋ go deo,
'Fad 's mairfeas aon laoċ, 'nn a ḃ-fuil tír-ċumann beo,
Le ḃeiṫ cosaint na g-ceart, d'a ḃ-fuil aige claon:
Béiḋ glóir aig fíor-ḟoilsiúġaḋ na h-áit', ḃ-fuil 'nna luiḋe
Na mairtiriḋe tíre, aig ar ḃris brón a g-croiḋe,
A ḃ-fad ó ċos claḋaire, nó tráill suaraiġ, daoir,
D'a ḃ-faire 's d'a g-cúṁdaċ aig na h-óig-ġaetiḃ saor,
Faoi 'n g-craoḃ-ola Spáinneaċ 'gus seamróg na ḃ-fian.

II.

If the fame of our fathers, bequeath'd with their rights,
Give to country its charm, and to home its delights,
  If deceit be a wound, and suspicion a stain,
Then, ye men of Iberia, our cause is the same,
And oh! may his tomb want a tear and a name,
Who would ask for a nobler, a holier death,
Than to turn his last sigh into victory's breath,
  For the Shamrock of Erin and Olive of Spain!

III.

Ye Blakes and O'Donnels, whose fathers resign'd
The green hills of their youth, among strangers to find
  That repose which, at home, they had sighed for in vain,
Join, join in our hope that the flame which you light
May be felt yet in Erin, as calm and as bright,
And forgive even Albion while blushing she draws,
Like a truant, her sword, in the long-slighted cause
  Of the Shamrock of Erin and Olive of Spain!

IV.

God prosper the cause!—oh, it cannot but thrive,
While the pulse of one patriot heart is alive,
  Its devotion to feel, and its rights to maintain.
Then, how sainted by sorrow its martyrs will die!
The finger of Glory shall point where they lie;
While, far from the footstep of coward or slave,
The young spirit of Freedom shall shelter their grave
  Beneath Shamrocks of Erin and Olives of Spain!

Mar an naoṁ-ṫeine lasta a g-Cill-dara Laiġean.

Fonn—Tá me 'mo ċodlaḋ.

I.

Mar an naoṁ-ṫeine lasta a g-Cill-dara Laiġean,
Gan múċaḋ tré bliaḋanta de ḋoineann ġeur, ġorg,
Tá an ċroiḋe, ḃiḋeas lán síonta geur', úr mar an t-éiḋean,
'S naċ g-cóṁnuiġeann 'na ḋiaiġ sin air, fuiġeall bróin, no lorg.
Eirinn! O Eirinn! mar súd tá go mór
Do spiorad aig briseaḋ ṫri ḋúḃan na n-deor.

II.

Tá na ríġaċta d 'eis claonaḋ ó árd ċríoċ a réim',
Agus neulta na h-oiḋċe aig teaċt air a g-cáil,
Tá Eire mar ġrian maiḋne aig éiriġe a g-céim
'S ní ḃéiḋ aon t slám d'a geur-ḃruid go gairid le fáġail.
Eirinn! O Eirinn! tá le saoġaltaiḃ faoi sgáṫ,
Nuair eulóċas a g-clú-san, béiḋ do ċaiṫréim faoi bláṫ.

III.

Ḃiḋeann an lile feaḋ geiṁriḋ 'n a codlaḋ sa g-cré,
Gan meaṫaḋ le bairleaċ, gan dúraċt le sion,
Go n-éiriġiḋ arís le gaeṫiḃ an earraiġ,
Fáġail ó ṫéagar na h-árd-ġréine fasgaḋ a's dion.
Eirinn! O Eirinn! tá do ġeiṁreaḋ faoi suan.
'S an dóiġ, a ṁair beó tríot, béiḋ bláṫaṁail go buan.

LIKE THE BRIGHT LAMP THAT SHONE.

Air—*Tha ma ma colla.*

I.

Like the bright lamp that shone in Kildare's holy fane,
And burn'd through long ages of darkness and storm,
Is the heart that sorrows have frown'd on in vain,
Whose spirit outlives them, unfading and warm.
Erin! O Erin! thus bright through the tears
Of a long night of bondage thy spirit appears.

II.

The nations have fallen, and thou still art young;
Thy sun is but rising, when others are set:
And tho' slavery's cloud o'er thy morning hath hung,
The full noon of freedom shall beam round thee yet.
Erin! O Erin! tho' long in the shade,
Thy star will shine out when the proudest shall fade.

III.

Unchill'd by the rain, and unwak'd by the wind,
The lily lies sleeping thro' winter's cold hour,
Till Spring's light touch her fetters unbind,
And daylight and liberty bless the young flower.
Thus Erin! O Erin! thy winter is past,
And the hope that liv'd through it shall blossom at last.

NA TOIG AIR AN B-FILE.

Fonn—Caitlin Tiriall.

I.

Na tóig air an ḃ-file, má euluiġeann fá'n g-cluan,
'N a m-bíḋeann roġ-ċlaon aig fonóid faoi árd-tuaḋ go buan,
Níor ċair ḃí ḋoiġ sinsir 's le uain 'gus le trá
Go clutaṁuil, do ḋéanfaḋ gníoṁ gáirgiḋ, gan sgáṫ
An teud, tá 'nois sínte air an g-ceol-ċruit go fann,
Do ṡeolfaḋ a g-croiḋe an náṁaid an bás-ġaṫ go teann;
'S an teanga, naċ sileann aċt mil-ṡruṫ na g-claon,
Ḃuḋ tuilteaċ í aig brosdúġaḋ gráḋa tíre na ḃ-Fian—

II.

Mo nuair d'a tír áluinn! tá a caiṫréim 'nn a luiḋe,
'S an croiḋe cróḋa briste, nár ḃ' féidir a ċlaoiḋeaḋ
Caiṫfiḋ éagcaoin a ṡíor-sliocṫ ḃeiṫ faluiġṫe ó'n t-saoġal,
'Oir is bás-ḃreiṫ a ċosaint, 's ní ḃ-fuil a cumann gan baoġal.
Tá a clan gan aon ċeannas, mar n-déanfaid siad feall,
'S mur d-truailliġid a sinsear aig iompóġaḋ le Gall;
'S an tsullsean, tá aig lasaḋ slíġe céime, gaċ lá,
Naċ sgiobṫar ó'n g-cárn é, air a ḃ-fuil Eire 'ga cráḋaḋ.

III.

Na tóig air an ḃ-file a ḃeiṫ aig síor-ḋéanaḋ rann,
'S an t-olc, naċ n-dán léiġeas, do ḋíbreaḋ le greann:
Ḃíḋeaḋ aige aċt leus dóċcuis, is lasfaiḋ go beo
A rosg tre ḃrat cúṁa mar an ġrian tre sgám ceo:
Déanfaiḋ íoḋbairt do Eirinn de na beusaiḃ, a ḃíḋeann
'Ga seolaḋ air mearḃall le fánaḋ a ċlaon,
'S le dlaoiġ na g-craoḃ glas, a tá fiġte air a ċeann
Mar an Greug, aig imirt díoġaltais, falóċaiḋ sé a lann.

IV.

Aċt giḋ gur ealuiġ do mór-ċéim, mar aisling na h-oiḋċe
Ḃéiḋiḋ d'ainm 'ga luaḋ aig an ḃ-file a ċoiḋċe,
An trá is mó suascas air a aigne le féin,
Ḃeiḋ aig seinnim go h-árd-ḃinn do leaṫtrom 's do leun:

OH! BLAME NOT THE BARD

AIR—*Kitty Tyrrell.*

I.

Oh! blame not the bard, if he fly to the bowers
  Where Pleasure lies carelessly smiling at Fame:
He was born for much more, and in happier hours
  His soul might have burn'd with a holier flame;
The string that now languishes loose o'er the lyre,
  Might have bent a proud bow to the warrior's dart;
And the lip which now breathes but the song of desire,
  Might have pour'd the full tide of a patriot's heart.

II.

But alas! for his country!—her pride has gone by,
  And that spirit is broken, which never would bend;
O'er the ruin her children in secret must sigh,
  For 't is treason to love her, and death to defend.
Unpriz'd are her sons till they 've learn'd to betray;
  Undistinguish'd they live, if they shame not their sires;
And the torch, that would light them thro' dignity's way,
  Must be caught from the pile where their country expires.

III.

Then blame not the bard, if in pleasure's soft dream
  He should try to forget what he never can heal;
Oh! give but a hope—let a vista but gleam
  Through the gloom of his country, and mark how he 'll feel!
That instant, his heart at her shrine would lay down,
  Every passion it nurs'd, every bliss it ador'd,
While the myrtle, now idly entwin'd with his crown,
  Like the wreath of Harmodius, should cover his sword.

IV.

But tho' glory be gone, and tho' hope fade away,
  Thy name, lovèd Erin, shall live in his songs:
Not ev'n in the hour, when his heart is most gay,
  Will he lose the remembrance of thee and thy songs.

Cluinfiḋ an coigríġeaċ do ġárṫa-ċroiḋe fíor,
Raċfaiḋ éagcaoin do ċláirsiġ ṫar muir a's ṫar tír,
'S do ṫiaġrnaiḋ, aig teannaḋ na slaḃraiḋe do d' ċlaoiḋ,
Silfiḋ deora na truaiġe le teann ḃrisde croiḋe.

SGALA LÍON DO'N MNAOI.

Fonn—Heig, h-óg!

I.

Sgála líon do'n mnaoi
D'a d-tug an bard gean mór,
An óig do ċeol ṫug gnaoi
Naċ d-taḃrfaḋ coiḋċe d' ór.
'O! rinneaḋ croiḋe mná sáṁ'
Do laṁaiḃ filiḋ grinn
Faoi ṁearaiḃ neaċ gan dáṁ
Ni ḃíḋeann se leaṫ ċo binn.
Sgála líon do'n mnaoi, etc.

II.

Ceistiġ Grean a's Sóġ
An Deise, aig glaine 'tiġe:
"B-fuil beallaċ 'steaċ,—cia do?"
"D' ar treise", ḟreagair sí.
D' iompuiġ an glaine an t-'Or,
Gan féiḋm le n 'oċair buiḋe,
B' Fearr sniṫeaḋ an Grean go mór
'Le a liaġ-ġeal 'gearraḋ ṫríḋ
Sgála líon, do'n mnaoi, etc.

The stranger shall hear thy lament on his plains;
  The sigh of thy harp shall be sent o'er the deep,
Till thy masters themselves, as they rivet thy chains,
  Shall pause at the song of their captive, and weep!

DRINK TO HER.

AIR—*Heigh, ho!*

I.

Drink to her who long
  Hath wak'd the poet's sigh,
The girl who gave to song
  What gold could never buy.
Oh! woman's heart was made
  For minstrel hands alone,
By other fingers play'd,
  It yields not half the tone.
Then here 's to her who long
  Hath wak'd the poet's sigh,
The girl who gave to song,
  What gold could never buy.

II.

At Beauty's door of glass
  When Wealth and Wit once stood,
They asked her, "Which might pass?"
  She answer'd, "He, who could".
With golden key Wealth thought
  To pass—but 't would not do:
While Wit a diamond brought,
  Which cut his bright way through.
So here 's to her who long
  Hath waked the poet's sigh,
The girl who gave to song
  What gold could never buy.

III.

An gean 'ḃíḋeas síos a' tnú,
  Le tiġṫe saiḃris móir,
Is samail é le cnúṁ
  Dal síos a g-claisiḃ óir;
Aċt suas do coṁnuiġeas grád
  An ḃaird measg reulta geal
Ci congḃuiġeann é gean mná
  Air talaṁ air feaḋ Seall
    Sgála líon do'n mnaoi, etc.

ROIṀ AN COGAḊ.

Fonn—Ríġ-ḃean na Síġe.

I.

Dar an dóiġ-ċroiḋe. a tá aig soilsiúġaḋ
  Dúinn-ne a máraċ brúiċ an ġleo;
Dar aġaiḋ na gréine, ḃeiḋeas aig soilsiuġaḋ
  Orainn, faon, no buaḋaċ, beo;
O! is fíor gur niḋ naċ fiú,
Ḃeiṫ beo, mar ḋaor-neaċ, gan aon ċlú—
  Mar an ġrian aig claonaḋ lae,
  Téiḋeann an laoċ ċum suain 's an g-cré
Lár trom-ġola ċreaḃ go leor:
  'S beannuiġṫe an té air ḃruaċ an t-saoġail,
  M-ḃíḋeann d'a ḃeoḋaḋan smuigiḋ gaoil,
D'a soilsiuġaḋ síos tre gleann na n-deor:
  Aċt ó! naċ breáġ do ṫéiḋid ċum sgiṫ,
  A ḃíḋeann air uċt na ḃuaḋa 'nn a luiḋe.

II.

Os cinn na n-eiḃleog, deis an ċeċ',
  Iompuiġeann leaca an náṁad bán,
Trá do ċuiṁníġeann air an maġ,
  Ann ar ṫuit faoi neull a ġlóir ḃí lán—

III.

The love that seeks a home
  Where wealth and grandeur shines,
Is like the gloomy gnome
  That dwells in dark gold mines.
But oh! the poet's love
  Can boast a brighter sphere;
Its native home 's above,
  Tho' woman keeps it here.
Then drink to her who long
  Hath wak'd the poet's sigh,
The girl who gave to song
  What gold could never buy.

BEFORE THE BATTLE.

AIR—*The Fairy Queen.*

I.

By the hope within us springing,
  Herald of to-morrow's strife;
By that sun, whose light is bringing
  Chains or freedom, death or life—
Oh! remember life can be
No charm for him who lives not free!
  Like the day-star in the wave
  Sinks a hero in his grave,
Midst the dew-fall of a nation's tears.
  Happy is he o'er whose decline
  The smiles of home may soothing shine,
And light him down the steep of years—
  But oh! how blest they sink to rest,
  Who close their eyes on victory's breast!

II.

O'er his watch-fire's fading embers,
  Now the foeman's cheek turns white,
When his heart that field remembers,
  Where we tam'd his tyrant might!

An slaḃra d'ḟásgaḋ arís go deo,
Do ḃriseamar, na léigiḋe ḋó
 Eisd, tá an t-aḋarc roiṁ oiḋċe aig blaoḋaċ
 Go h-árd ċum briste air gaċ laoċ—
Líontar suas an ċuaċ go ceann;
 Is iomḋa neaċ anois treun, roiṁ oiḋċe,
 Ḃeiḋeas cuġṫa air an ḃ-faiṫ 'nn a luiḋe,
'S naċ n-dúisgfiḋ gáir na buaiḋe teann';
 Aċt ó! naċ beannuiġṫe bás an luain,
 A ṫéiḋeas le gol an t-saoġail ċum suain.

ṪUIT AIR AN M-BUAḊARG SLAM NA H-OIḊĊE.

Fonn—D' uċt ḟionn.

I.

Ṫuit air an m-buaḋarg slám na h-oiḋċe,
 Agus d'ḟoilsiġ teinteaċ bár na m-beann,
'Nn a raiḃ laoċra treun' 's an ár 'nna luiḋe,
 'S air ḟan ḋioḃ beo, neaṁ-eaglaċ, fann!
Naċ boċt an sgeul, tuar briste croiḋe!
 Sár-ḋóiġ gaisgiḋeaċ beiṫ faoi lár—
D'éis caill, a's creaċ gaċ uile niḋ
 Aċt beaṫa aṁain a's cliu 's an ár.

II.

Buḋ mall 's buḋ trom ḃi teaċt an trá,
 A d'ḟair na fir le imniḋe cruaiḋ,
Go soilseoċaḋ orrṫa arís an lá,
 'Nn a ḃ-fuiġfeaḋ go cinte bás no buaiḋ:
Ta saoġal, naċ m-biḋeann an fóirne daor,
 Naċ g-cleaċtann geur-ḟlat tiġearnaiḋ dian;
Má 's bearna an bás ċum an t-saoġail úd saor,
 Mo ṫruaiġe do 'n sglaḃaiḋe beo faoi leun.

Never let him bind again
A chain, like that we broke from then.
  Hark! the horn of combat calls—
  Ere the golden evening falls,
May we pledge that horn in triumph round!
  Many a heart that now beats high,
  In slumber cold at night shall lie,
Nor waken even at victory's sound—
  But oh! how blest that hero's sleep,
  O'er whom a wond'ring world shall weep!

AFTER THE BATTLE.

AIR—*Thy Fair Bosom.*

I.

Night clos'd around the conqueror's way,
  And lightnings show'd the distant hill,
Where those who lost that dreadful day
  Stood few and faint, but fearless still!
The soldier's hope, the patriot's zeal,
  For ever dimm'd, for ever crost—
Oh! who shall say what heroes feel,
  When all but life and honour 's lost?

II.

The last sad hour of freedom's dream,
  And valour's task, mov'd slowly by,
While mute they watch'd till morning's beam
  Should rise and give them light to die.
There 's yet a world where souls are free,
  Where tyrants taint not nature's bliss;
If death that world's bright opening be,
  Oh! who would live a slave in this?

D'ÉIS FAD-SIÚḂAIL TRÍ SAOĠAL CRUAIḊ, CAM.

Fonn—Bruaċa na Banna.

I.

D'éis fad-siúḃail trí saoġal cruaiḋ cam,
'Gur caill' ar g-cáirde, céime 's mear'
Is áil linn ceol, le 'r éist 'san am,
Raiḃ fós gaċ niḋ fa snuaḋ 's fa snás.
O! naċ fáiltaṁail fuaim gaċ rinn,
Dúraċt smuainte, ċuaiḋ faoi ċaṁ
'S aig lasaḋ le n-a gaeṫiḃ binn'
Smigeaḋ a suiliḃ ḃí faoi slám.

II.

Mar gaeṫe aig téaċt trí fásaċ bláṫ,
'N oir ó ċrícib grianṁar' teo,
Bíḋeas an ceol, do cluinfiḋe, trá
Raiḃ teagar againn, seun a's sóg:
D'éis gaċ bláṫ ḃeiṫ críon 'nna luiḋe
Bíḋeann a ḃalaḋ beo air an gaoṫ go fóill;
Mar súd, d'éis eug, do'n t-siansa 'coiḋċe,
Tig a ṫais' arís air gaeṫiḃ ceoil.

III.

A g-coṁear ceoil tá beurla fann
'S an teanga is tuilteiġe fós gan ḃriġ!
Ní'l aċt draoiḋeaċt ceolṁar rann
Foilsiġeas smuainte a's rúin an ċroiḋe.
Bíḋeann focla cáirdis de ġliocas lán,
Is breugaiġ fós iad briaṫara an ġráḋa;
Ní'l aċt gaeṫe ceolta dán,
Beir ciúnas síor gan feall, gan cráḋ.

ON MUSIC.

Air—The Banks of Banna.

I.

When thro' life unblest we rove,
  Losing all that made life dear,
Should some notes we us'd to love
  In days of boyhood, meet our ear,
Oh! how welcome breathes the strain!
  Wakening thoughts that long have slept,
Kindling former smiles again,
  In faded eyes that long have wept.

II.

Like the gale that sighs along
  Beds of oriental flowers,
Is the grateful breath of song
  That once was heard in happier hours.
Fill'd with balm, the gale sighs on,
  Though the flowers have sunk in death;
So, when pleasure's dream is gone,
  Its memory lives in Music's breath.

III.

Music! oh! how faint, how weak,
  Language fades before thy spell!
Why should Feeling ever speak,
  When thou canst breathe her soul so well?
Friendship's balmy words may feign;
  Love's are ev'n more false than they;
Oh! 't is only Music's strain
  Can sweetly soothe, and not betray!

NÍ LEIS NA DEORAIḂ, DO SILTEAR SA TRÁ.

Fonn—Na sé piġin.

I.

Ní leis na deoraiḃ, do siltear sa tra,
  A sintear é a g-cré na h-uaiṁe,
Taisbeantar teas agus téagar ar n-gráḋa,
  No doiṁnear dorċa ar g-cúṁa:
Aċt le deoraiḃ aig teaċt go síor-fuar o'n g-croiḋe,
  Foilsiġtear gur buan ar smuainte
Air an m-bás, a scap dúḃan air aoiḃneas ar m-biṫ,
  D'ar b-fágail mar deoraiḋṫe claoiḋte.

II.

Có-ḟad a's beiḋeas a beaṫa glas ann ar g-croiḋe,
  A's a ḃás, mar is dual, 'g a ċaoineaḋ,
Beiḋ a beusa mar lóċrann sgeiṫ solais air ar slíġe
  'Gus ar d-toil ċum gaċ maiṫeasa aig claonaḋ—
Mar an deaġ-ḃalaḋ taiṫneaṁaċ, beireas an fuiġeall,
  Do'n úir, a m-bíḋean Naoiṁ ann sínte,
Beiḋ a ċáiliḋeaċt ann ar g-cuiṁne gaċ lá d'ar saoġal
  'S ar g-croiḋe le n-a iomáiġ, líonta.

GIḊ 'S TROM SLÁM AR M-BUAḊARṪA.

Fonn—La Féile Naoiṁ Patraic.

I.

Giḋ 's trom slám ar m-buaḋarṫa, ní aireóċam' an iuḋ é,
  Béiḋ ar n-gáirdeas trí ḋeóra mar ġaċ gréine a síon,
Níor cruṫuiġeaḋ riaṁ croiḋṫe, mar m-beiḋeaḋ cruas air riġṫe,
  Buḋ cumannaiġe beusa 's buḋ téagaraiġe claon!

IT IS NOT THE TEAR AT THIS MOMENT SHED.

AIR—*The Sixpence.*

I.

It is not the tear at this moment shed,
  When the cold turf has just been laid o'er him,
That can tell how beloved was the friend that 's fled,
  Or how deep in our hearts we deplore him.
'T is the tear, thro' many a long day wept,
  'T is life's whole path o'ershaded;
'T is the one remembrance, fondly kept,
  When all lighter griefs have faded.

II.

Thus his memory, like some holy light,
  Kept alive in our hearts, will improve them,
For worth shall look fairer, and truth more bright,
  When we think how he liv'd but to love them.
And, as fresher flowers the sod perfume
  Where buried saints are lying,
So our hearts shall borrow a sweet'ning bloom
  From the image he left there in dying.

THE PRINCE'S DAY.

AIR—*Saint Patrick's Day.*

I.

Tho' dark are our sorrows, to-day we 'll forget them,
  And smile through our tears, like a sunbeam in showers,
There never were hearts, if our rulers would let them,
  More formed to be grateful and blest than ours.

Aċt, faraoir! sa trá,
A n-úruiġeann an bláṫ,
Aig falaċ na slaḃraiḋe, a ċráḋ sinn go teann;
Bíḋeann aig fásgaḋ gan sgiṫ
Lúb eile air ar g-croiḋe,
Tá ar suaircas, mar ṡolus aig mol-ċinn na cruinne,
Sgáil Lóċrainn lár dúḃain, ro ġeal lé ḃeiṫ buan,
'S dá m-b'e an eibleóg déiġionaċ air lá so na luinne,
Corróċaiḋ féile naoiṁ Pátruic é as a ṡuan.

II.

Mo ġráine air do loċtóiriḋ breugaċ', neaṁ-ṡaoiṫeaṁla;
Giḋ garg lé d' náṁaid, lé d' ċaraid táir fíor,
'S ní'l urram ċo taiṫneaṁaċ do neaċ air biṫ ríġaṁail,
Lé cumann ó'n g-croiḋe, le ar ail a ḃeiṫ saor.
Trá ḃeiḋeaḋ luċt sladta do ċliú
Is do ċeirt, tá leis dluṫ,
Mar ċlaḋairiḋ aig teiṫeaḋ ó ḃorb-ṫeas an gleó,
Beiḋeaḋ do ġlas-ḃrat ó'n g-crann
Ard sgaoilte go teann.
Dar mo ḋeas-láiṁ! da n-glaoḋfaiḋe anois tú ċum caṫa,
Do ṫraoṫfaḋ an ḟearg ann do ċroiḋe stiġ go ḃeó;
Is ḃeiḋeaḋ lorg ríġe Eireann go trom air do ṁaġaiḃ,
Aig treasgairt na náṁ a's 'g a sineaḋ a g-cró

III.

Gráḋuiġeann sé a glas-tír le gean, tá mar leaċta
Go doiṁin a g-croiḋṫiḃ, fuair casgairt 's cráḋ;
'S ḃéiḋ a ċoinġioll 's a ċumann faoi ċaoiṁṫeaċt cóir reaċta
'S béiḋ aoiḃneas Eireann go fóill fá ḃláṫ
Air a g-cloċ-seoide cruaiḋ
Beir síor-ḃuilliḋ buaiḋ.
Aċt ní ṫruailliġeann an lannair, tá stiġ lasta beó;
Do'n ċloiċ d'éis a brúġaḋ,
Beir an sgealpog is luġa
A Lóċrann: is, Eirinn, giḋ brista faoi creaċtaiḃ,
Tá teiṫ-splanc taoḃ stiġ díot, naċ muċfar go deo,
A ḃeoḋuiġeas gaċ ball, tabairt dó, luṫ a's eaċta
'S ḃeir air ḟéile Naoiṁ Pátruic dúinn gáirdeas a's sóġ.

But just when the chain
Has ceas'd to pain,
And hope has enwreath'd it round with flowers,
There comes a new link
Our spirits to sink—
Oh! the joy that we taste, like the light of the poles,
Is a flash amid darkness, too brilliant to stay:
But, though 't were the last little spark in our souls,
We must light it up now, on our Prince's Day,

II.

Contempt on the minion who calls you disloyal!
Tho' fierce to your foe, to your friends you are true;
And the tribute most high to a head that is royal,
Is love from a heart that loves liberty too.
While cowards who blight
Your fame, your right,
Would shrink from the blaze of the battle array,
The standard of Green
In front would be seen—
Oh! my life on your faith! were you summon'd this minute,
You 'd cast every bitter remembrance away,
And show what the arm of old Erin has in it,
When roused by the foe, on her Prince's Day.

III.

He loves the Green Isle, and his love is recorded
In hearts which have suffer'd too much to forget;
And hope shall be crown'd, and attachment rewarded,
And Erin's gay jubilee shine out yet.
The gem may be broke
By many a stroke
But nothing can cloud its native ray.
Each fragment will cast
A light to the last,—
And thus, Erin, my country, tho' broken thou art,
There 's a lustre within thee that ne'er will decay;
A spirit which beams through each suffering part,
And now smiles at all pain on the Prince's Day.

GUILIḊ, GUILIḊ.

Fonn—Aḃran an Ḃróin.

I.

Guiliḋ, Guiliḋ deóra a ṡruṫ,
Cuaiḋ ḃur n-am ṫart mar ċeó ;
Tá ḃur m-baill gan lúṫ ó ċuiḃriġ tiuġ'
'S ni ḃéiḋ ḃur ḃ-fir níos mó!
Buḋ díoṁaoin gairge laoċra teann
Buḋ díoṁaoin cóṁairle ciallṁar faoi:
'S gaċ áit d'a múċtar saoirse ann,
Ni lasann arís a ċoiḋċe.

II.

Guiliḋ: go fóill do déanfar ceart,
Le staraiḃ Innse Fáil
'S air iomad eáċt do ṡoillseóċar cairt,
Tá anois faoi smúid dúiḃ cáil'
'S aig siúḃal doiḃ tír, do fágaḋ bán,
Ḃ-fuil an t-osc 's an tráill 'sa n-uaiṁ,
Cia an dóiġ, le íongnaḋ ḟiafróċas, lan,
Ḃ-fuáir díoġa air sgaiṫ, suaiṁ buaiḋ?

III.

"Is cineaṁain ċruaiḋ (beiḋid 'g a luaḋ),
Rinne oige ḃur n-imris a ḋealḃ:
'S nuair ḃí ḃur náṁ dlúṫ, teann a ḃ-fuaṫ,
Níor ġlac grāḋ oraiḃ sealḃ:
Aċt d'ḟuaruiġ croiḋċe buḋ dual ḃeiṫ teiṫ,
Aig truailliuġaḋ Dé na m-beannaċt,
'S air ċill, do ṫaṫuiġ roinn fá leiṫ,
Do ṫaosg roinn eile mallaċt".

WEEP ON, WEEP ON.

AIR—*The Song of Sorrow.*

I.

Weep on, weep on, your hour is past;
  Your dreams of pride are o'er:
The fatal chain is round you cast,
  And you are men no more.
In vain the hero's heart hath bled;
  The sage's tongue hath warn'd in vain:—
O Freedom! once thy flame hath fled,
  It never lights again.

II.

Weep on: perhaps in after days
  They 'll learn to love your name:
When many a deed may wake in praise
  That long hath slept in blame.
And when they tread the ruin'd aisle
  Where rest, at length, both lord and slave,
They 'll wondering ask how hands so vile
  Could conquer hearts so brave?

III.

"'T was fate", they 'll say, "a wayward fate,
  Your web of discord wove;
And while your tyrants joined in hate,
  You never joined in love.
But hearts fell off that ought to twine,
  And man profan'd what God had given,
Till some were heard to curse the shrine
  Where others knelt to heaven".

SINSIORAĊT AN ĊLAIRSIĠ.

Fonn—Gang Fane.

I.

Ta iompaḋ gur suiriḋ do ċoṁnuiġ fa 'n toinn,
Do ḃi anns an g-cruit so 'nois duisġim go binn,
Ḃiḋeaḋ aig eulóġaḋ o' n ṁuir geal le linn teaċt na h-oiḋċe,
Cum na tráiġe aig óglaċ air a raiḃ aici gnaoi.

II.

Aċt buḋ diṁaoin a cúram, óir d' ḟag í gaċ oiḋċe,
Aig tomaḋ ann a deoraiḃ a folt Fáineaċ, buiḋe;
Gur ḋearc neaṁ le truaiġe air ḟuiriḋ na d-tonn,
Dí déanaḋ 'nna cláirseaċ so saṁ taḃ'rt fonn.

III.

Buḋ dear fós a h-uċt, as air 'gruaiḋ snoḋ do las,
'S máise tuillseaċ na mara, air a cum ṫart do ċas
'Ġus a folt silt na n-deor le raiḃ taisleaċ o 'n t-sruṫ
Tuit a nuas air an g-clár, déanaḋ teud' na m-binn-guṫ.

IV.

Ann aonḟeaċt go g-cluistear, o'n g-clairseaċ, so an saċ,
Fuaim measgṫa cumaoin 'gus cuṁa sa' trá,
Go n-dearnis d 'a n-dealbuġaḋ ó ċeile dá roinn
Ceol géantraċ, is me garr duit;—'s me a g-cian,—guiltreaċ, binn.

THE ORIGIN OF THE HARP.

AIR—*Gage Fane.*

I.

'T is believed that this Harp, which I wake now for thee,
Was a Siren of old, who sung under the sea,
And who often, at eve, thro' the bright waters rov'd,
To meet on the green shore a youth whom she lov'd.

II.

But she lov'd him in vain, for he left her to weep,
And in tears, all the night, her gold tresses to steep,
Till Heaven look'd with pity on true love so warm,
And chang'd to this soft Harp the sea-maiden's form.

III.

Still her bosom rose fair—still her cheeks smil'd the same—
While the sea-beauties gracefully form'd the light frame;
And her hair, as, let loose, o'er her light form it fell,
Was chang'd to bright chords, uttering melody's spell.

IV.

Hence it came, that this soft Harp so long hath been known
To mingle love's language with sorrow's sad tone;
Till *thou* didst divide them and teach the fond lay
To speak love when I 'm near thee, and grief when away!

A n-gleann an Duḃ-Loċa 's le n-a taoḃ.

Fonn—An Cailín donn Eirionnaċ.

I.

A n-gleann an Duḃ-Loċa 's le n-a ṫaoḃ,
'N áit nár ṡeinn fuiseog fós a riaṁ,
Air ḃár árd aille, os cionn an ċuain,
Ċuaiḋ naoṁ Caoiṁġein óg ċum suain.
" An ḃean, tá air mo ṫóir, ní ḃ-fuiġiḋ
" An áit so, m-béiḋ me, feasd' mo luiḋe".
Faraor! is beag do ṫuig sa trá
Sé cluain a's cleasa ṁeallṫoċ' mná.

II.

Sí Cáit óg, na n-gorm-súl,
A ċuir air teiṫeaḋ, é, 's ċum siuḃal;
Ḃuḋ ḃuan a gráḋ. 's níor ċoir léi é,
A ḃeiṫ 'nna céile aig giolla Dé.
Cia air biṫ áit ar ġluais an naoṁ,
Ċluin sé a coiscéim le n-a ṫaoḃ;
Téiḋeaḋ soir no siar, de ló, nó d'oiḋċe
Casfaiḋ a súil leis annsa t-sliġe.

III.

Air ḃár na creige anois 'nn a luiḋé,
Téiḋ se ċum suaimnis a's ċum sgíṫ.
Aig smuaineaḋ air neaṁ, gan cás, gan cráḋ
Fá ḃeiṫ ó ċaṫuġaḋ mná faoi sgáṫ.
Aċt ní'l aon ċlúid, no cláis, faraor!
O ġaċṫiḃ mná, tá ceanaṁail, saor:
Fad tá 'nn a ċodlaḋ feuċ 'sa trá
Cáit aig silt na n-deor lé gráḋ.

BY THAT LAKE WHOSE GLOOMY SHORE.

AIR—*The brown Irish girl.*

I.

By that lake, whose gloomy shore
Sky-lark never warbles o'er,
Where the cliff hangs high and steep,
Young Saint Kevin stole to sleep.
"Here at least", he calmly said,
"Woman ne'er shall find my bed".
Ah! the good Saint little knew
What the wily sex can do.

II.

'T was from Kathleen's eyes he flew,—
Eyes of most unholy blue!
She had lov'd him well and long,
Wish'd him hers, nor thought it wrong.
Wheresoe'er the Saint would fly,
Still he heard her light foot nigh;
East or west, where'er he turn'd,
Still her eyes before him burn'd.

III.

On the bold cliff's bosom cast,
Tranquil now he sleeps at last;
Dreams of Heav'n, nor thinks that e'er
Woman's smile can haunt him there.
But nor earth nor heav'n is free
From her power, if fond she be.
Even now, while calm he sleeps,
Kathleen o'er him leans and weeps.

IV.

Gan eagla gáḋa trí creaga gorg',
Go cuas na h-aille lean sí a lorg,
Is 'nuair do ḋealruiġ bán an lae,
D' ḟoilsiġ sgéiṁ a dreaċ 's a gné.
Is cruaiḋ an croiḋe, a tá aig na naoiṁ;
'Oir d'éis a h-airuġaḋ le n-a ṫaob,
Do leim go deifreaċ ó n-a ḟáṁ.
Is ċeilg le fánaḋ í, sa t-snáṁ.

V.

A láir do linne, a Ġleann-dá-loċ,
Ṫuit Cáit le glasaḋ an lae go moċ.
Do ṁaoḋam go mall é truaiġe do 'n ṁnaoi,
A d'eug tre grád 's tre seaċmall croiḋe—
Tra ġuiḋ d'a h-anam beaṫa ḟuṫain,
Do cloisead ceol air ḟad an ċuain,
Le a raib na cnoic 's na gleanta binn,
'Nuair a d'eiriġ a taise geal ó'n tuinn.

ṪUIT LANN LONNRAĊ EIREANN.

Fonn—Cruaċán na Féine.

I.

Ṫuit lann lonnraċ Eireann le builliḋe luaṫa, geur-tiuġ'
Air an té, ḃraiṫ clann Uisniġ a's ḃris geallaḋ an riġ:
'S ní lia braon goirt gola, a falcaḋ ó'n ḃ-feall duḃ,
'Ná sgársfar air a cloiḋeaṁ ó sruṫ fola a ċroiḋe.

II.

Dar an dearg-lám, ḃí os cionn Lann-duḃ Concoḃair aig síneaḋ,'
'Nuair ḃí trí laoċra Ulaiḋ a leaba fola faoi suan:
Dar na treun-tonna caṫa aig borraḋ 's aig lionaḋ
A feól na gaisgiḋiġ go buaḋac, 's go treisaṁail ċum cuain.

IV.

Fearless she had track'd his feet
To this rocky, wild retreat;
And, when morning met his view,
Her mild glances met it too.
Ah! your Saints have cruel hearts!
Sternly from his bed he starts,
And, with rude, repulsive shock,
Hurl'd her from the beetling rock.

V.

Glendalough! thy gloomy wave
Soon was gentle Kathleen's grave!
Soon the Saint (yet ah! too late)
Felt her love, and mourn'd her fate.
When he said, "Heav'n rest her soul!"
Round the Lake light music stole;
And her ghost was seen to glide,
Smiling, o'er the fatal tide!

AVENGING AND BRIGHT.

Air—*Crochan of the Irish Fenii or Militia.*

I.

Avenging and bright fall the swift sword of Erin
On him who the brave sons of Usna betray'd—
For every fond eye he hath waken'd a tear in,
A drop from his heart-wounds shall weep o'er her blade.

II.

By the red cloud that hung over Conor's dark dwelling,
When Ulad's three champions lay sleeping in gore—
By the billows of war, which so often, high swelling,
Have wafted these heroes to victory's shore—

III.

Móidiġmuid cúitiuġaḋ: ó ṡianṡ' ḃíḋmuid falaṁ:
Bíḋeaḋ an óiġ gan céile, bíḋeaḋ an ċruit gan ceol, fann;
Bíḋeaḋ an teallaċ gan suaircas, 's gan saoṫruġaḋ an talaṁ;
Go g-cáirnṫear trom-ḋíoġoltas anuas air a ċeann.

IV.

A Ríġ! giḋ gur milis ar m-baile do ṁeabruġaḋ;
Giḋ gur taiṫneaṁaċ na deora do siltear le dáiṁ:
Giḋ gur aoibinn gaċ gean air luċt cáirdais a's cabro,
Le díoġaltas air dian-olc ní 'l aon niḋ ċó sáiṁ.

TÁ AN SAOĠAL SO LÉIR-ṀEASGṪA.

Fonn—Dual na b-fead glas.

I.

Tá an saoġal so léir-ṁeasgṫa le buaiḋreaḋ 's le sog
A ruaigeas a ċéile mar ṫonna na ṡraiġ':
'S ar súile, aig silt deor, no le gáirdeaċas beo,
Mar na toinn, ṫig go duḃ, no go lonnraċ air tráiġ:
Bíḋeann ar g-cleasa aig teaċt d'éis ar n-anró ċo tiuġ
Go g-cluintear an gáiré roiṁ trumuġaḋ na súl;
'S ní luaiṫe do siltear an braon truaiġe le bruṫ
'Ná ċumaileann é, cleite na baoise air siúbal,
Aċt suid ort: ní ḟanfaiḋ aon blas air an t-saoġal,
Le ceannaiḃ síor-ċríonna,'s le croiḋṫiḃ síor-beo,
Air ar g-crann, líḋeaḋ an lag-brón tá le gáirdeas a n-gaol
'S an luinne bíḋeas loinnreaċ, geárr-ṡaoġlaċ go deo.

III.

We swear to revenge them!—no joy shall be tasted,
  The harp shall be silent, the maiden unwed,
Our halls shall be mute and our fields shall lie wasted,
  Till vengeance is wreak'd on the murderer's head!

IV.

Yes, monarch! though sweet are our home recollections,
  Though sweet are the tears that from tenderness fall;
Though sweet are our friendships, our hopes, our affections,
  Revenge on a tyrant is sweetest of all!

THIS LIFE IS ALL CHEQUER'D.

AIR—*The Bunch of Green Rushes.*

I.

This life is all chequer'd with pleasures and woes,
  That chase one another like waves of the deep—
Each brightly or darkly, as onward it flows,
  Reflecting our eyes as they sparkle or weep.
So closely our whims on our miseries tread,
  That the laugh is awak'd ere the tear can be dried;
And, as fast as the rain-drop of Pity is shed,
  The goose-plumage of Folly can turn it aside.
But pledge me the cup—if existence would cloy,
  With hearts ever happy and heads ever wise,
Be ours the light Sorrow, half-sister to Joy,
  And the light brilliant Folly that flashes and dies.

II.

'Nuair a cuireaḋ an t-óglaċ le foiġteaċ ċum sruṫ',
Trí maġa glas' grianṁar', gan brón air a ċroiḋe;
Do b' aerac a súile agus b' áluinn a ċruṫ,
'N áit dualgais, ag cruinniuġaḋ na m-bláṫ air an t-sliġe.
Mar súd tá, mar me, dream d'ár ḋual dóib líonaḋ
Ar sruṫ an fíor-coluir, tá líonṁar, neaṁ-ġan,
Tiomsúġaḋ na m-bláṫ, ċaiṫ an lá fada ag síneaḋ
A láiṁe: 's a soiṫeaċ gan braon air biṫ ann.
Aċt súd ort! 'nuair cruinniġeas an díoṁaoineas bláṫ
Le crúin-ḟleasg a ḋealḃ, ma ṫuiteann aon ḃraon
'O ṫobar na h-eagna air ḋuilleog sa trá,
Go cinte, béiḋ sásta, gan ceasaċt, mo ṁian.

TRÍḊ INNIS FÁIL.

Fonn—Aiblin Crócar.

I.

Tríḋ Innis-Fáil,
Ag rinceaḋ 'n 'dáil
Trá ġluais gráḋ 'gus gairge
'Gus ríġ 'n ġrún ġéir
Siuḃal leo 'sa ḃ-feur
'Sceiṫ gaeṫe ó n-a ṫairge
Air feaḋ na sliġe
Tig feur tri-ḋlaoiġe
Faoi ḋruċta dealra, falcuiġṫe
'Gur é ċo glas
Le Smarog deas
Tríḋ scáṫán crístil calcuiġṫe
An t-seamróg, tá glas síor-buan an t-seamróg!
De ḋuilleóg sgaiṫ,
Ag file 's flaiṫ,
Fás Eire' aṁáin an t-seamróg!

II.

When Hylas was sent with his urn to the fount,
Thro' fields full of light, with heart full of play,
Light rambled the boy over meadow and mount,
And neglected his task for the flowers on the way.
Thus many, like me, who in youth should have tasted
The fountain that runs by Philosophy's shrine,
Their time with the flowers on the margin have wasted,
And left their light urns all as empty as mine.
But pledge me the goblet—while Idleness weaves
These flowerets together, should Wisdom but see
One bright drop or two that has fall'n on the leaves
From her fountain divine, 't is sufficient for me.

OH! THE SHAMROCK!

Air—*The Shamrock.*

I.

Through Erin's Isle,
To sport awhile,
As Love and Valour wander'd,
With Wit, the sprite,
Whose quiver bright
A thousand arrows squander'd;
Where'er they pass,
A triple grass
Shoots up, with dew-drops streaming,
As softly green
As emerald seen
Thro' purest crystal gleaming.
Oh! the Shamrock, the green, immortal Shamrock!
Chosen leaf
Of Bard and Chief,
Old Erin's native Shamrock!

II.

Aig gairge, aig ráḋ,
"'S dam tá faoi ḃláṫ,
"Na seoiḋe maiḋne craoḃaṁail',
"Ní h-aṁla tá",
Do ḟreagair gráḋ,
"Le m' ḟearan-s' an dil' aoiḃeaṁail";
Aċt ḋearc 'sa ḃ-feur
Trí ḋlaoiġ 'n t-síġ ġeur,
Gur' ġair air fead na sréire:
"Na sgoiltiḋ an bláṫ,
"Ta 's tnúir mar scáṫ,
"Gráḋ, gairge 's grean na h-Eire!"
O an t-seamróg, ta glas, sír-ḃúan, an t-seamróg!
De ḋuilleog sgaiṫ,
Aig file 's flaiṫ,
Fás Eire aṁáin an t-seamróg!

III.

Co dílis, fíor,
Ḃiḋeaḋ teann go síor
An ċuing an lá úd 'ċeangail,
'S air eite an ġaiṫ,
Na tuiteaḋ daṫ,
An domḃlais, nó a ṡaṁail!
Glanaḋ do h-eug,
An gráḋ ḋrís breug,
O an ngort tá faoi n a ṁaorsaċt,
'S ná tóigeaḋ go deo,
A ḃrat sa ngleo,
Gairge 'n agaiḋ na saorsaċt':
O an t-seamróg, ta glas, sin-ḃuan, an t-seamróg!
De ḋuilleog sgaiṫ,
Aig file 's flaiṫ,
Fás Eire' aṁáin an t-seamróg!

II.

Says Valour, "See,
"They spring for me,
"Those leafy gems of morning!"
Says Love, "No, no,
"For me they grow,
"My fragrant path adorning".
But Wit perceives
The triple leaves,
And cries, "Oh! do not sever
"A type that blends
"Three godlike friends,
"Love, Valour, Wit, for ever!"
Oh! the Shamrock, the green, immortal Shamrock!
Chosen leaf
Of Bard and Chief,
Old Erin's native Shamrock!

III.

So firmly fond
May last the bond
They wove that morn together,
And ne'er may fall
One drop of gall
On Wit's celestial feather!
May Love, as twine
His flowers divine,
Of thorny falsehood weed 'em!
May Valour ne'er
His standard rear
Against the cause of Freedom!
Oh! the Shamrock, the green, immortal Shamrock!
Chosen leaf
Of Bard and Chief,
Old Erin's native Shamrock!

AON ĊUAĊOG AṀÁIN AIG AN DORAS.

Fonn—Mol Ruaḋ na maidne.

I.

Aon ċuaċog aṁáin aig an doras
D'eis an iomad ċuaiḋ ċart air an g-clár,
'S an ċuaċ is mo cúṁa, gan foras
Is dual fós a líonaḋ go bárr.
Ta súarcas mor-ṡiansaṁail an t-saoġail so
Co mál a's ċo trom 'teaċt cum ċinn,
Naċ n' airiġtear aċt 'n-eis a ḋul síos ḋo
An t-aoibneas ḃí lé n-a linn:
Aċt de ṁóméid mar súd bíḋeaḋ ar m-beaṫa
'Ga ḋealḃaḋ go tiuġ, dlúṫ go leór,
Do ṫig as uċt sians' lé luas raṫa,
'Gur éagas 's a g-cuaċ a lár deor.

II.

Aig siúḃal ḋuinn air aġaiḋ, naċ claonṁar,
Geárr scíṫ do ġlacaḋ 'sa' tra,
Air ḃáinseaċ mar so áluinn grianṁar,
Ḃíḋeas lár o'n tor-ḟásaiġ faoi ḃláṫ.
Aċt deifriuġ, ḃíḋeann am 'ḃlaoḋaċ a ċoiḋċe,
Geur ġreadaḋ na n-uaire gan scíṫ,
Sé 's samail dó aisdear na gaoiṫe,
'Nuair a measg bláṫ ḃíḋeas a slíġ.
Aċt de ṁóméid mar sud bíḋeaḋ ar m-beaṫa
'Ga ḋealḃaḋ go tiuġ dluṫ go leór,
Do ṫig as uċt sians' le luas raṫa,
'Gur eagas 's a g-cuaċ a lár deor.

ONE BUMPER AT PARTING.

AIR—*Moll Roe in the morning.*

I.

One bumper at parting!—tho' many
Have circled the board since we met,
The fullest, the saddest of any
Remains to be crown'd by us yet.
The sweetness that pleasure hath in it
Is always so slow to come forth,
That seldom, alas! till the minute
It dies, do we know half its worth.
But come—may our life's happy measure
Be all of such moments made up;
They 're born on the bosom of Pleasure,
They die 'midst the tears of the cup.

II.

As onward we journey, how pleasant
To pause and inhabit awhile
Those few sunny spots, like the present,
That 'mid the dull wilderness smile!
But Time, like a pitiless master,
Cries "Onward!" and spurs the gay hours—
Ah, never doth time time travel faster
Than when his way lies among flowers.
But come—may our life's happy measure
Be all of such moments made up;
They 're born on the bosom of Pleasure,
They die 'midst the tears of the cup.

III.

Naċ soilseaċ do ḃí an ġrian aig claonaḋ
  Naċ dealraċ do ḋearc an ṁuir faoi?
Mar súd, 's dúal gaċ sleaḋ aig faonaḋ,
  Ḃeiṫ mar réalt an lae dul 'nna luiḋe.
Do ċonnairc mar ċruoċnuiġ se aisdear,
  Aig téilgan a ġaeṫe faoi ṫonn,
'S a lán ċuaiċ mar súd lonnraċ bastar
  Roiṁ scáraḋ ar g-cruinnuġaḋ le fonn
Aċt de ṁóméid mar súd brúḋeaḋ ar m-beaṫa
  'S a dealḃaḋ go tiuġ dlúṫ go leór,
Do ṫig as uċt sians' le luas raṫa,
  'Gus cugas 's a g-cuaċ a lár deor.

TÁ RÓS DEIĠIONAĊ AN T-SAṀRAIḊ.

Fonn—Coillte Blárna.

I.

Tá rós déiġionaċ an t-saṁraiḋ leis féin air an g-craoḃ,
D'eis a ċoṁluċt na sgeiṁe ḃeiṫ cugṫa air gaċ taoḃ:
Gan aon rós aṁáin gaolṁar, gan bláṫ, le a b-fuil dáiṁ,
Le lasaḋ, no osnaḋ ṫaḃairt air ais dó, go sáiṁ.

II.

Ní ḟágfad leat féin tú lé meaḋaḋ air an geug,
Gan do ṫeilgean a ċodlaḋ measg do ġaolta go h-eug:
'Náit a m-béiḋir fearda gaċ lá a's gaċ oiḋċe,
Leis na rósaiḃ gan bláṫ a's gan balaḋ do luiḋe

III.

We saw how the sun look'd in sinking,
The waters beneath him how bright,
And now let our farewell of drinking
Resemble that farewell of light.
You saw how he finished, by darting
His beam o'er a dark billow's brim—
So, fill up, let 's shine at our parting,
In full, liquid glory, like him.
And oh! may our life's happy measure
Of moments like this be made up;
'T was born on the bosom of Pleasure,
It dies 'mid the tears of the cup.

'T IS THE LAST ROSE OF SUMMER.

AIR—*The Groves of Blarney.*

I.

'T is the last rose of summer
Left blooming alone;
All her lovely companions
Are faded and gone;
No flower of her kindred,
No rose-bud is nigh,
To reflect back her blushes,
To give sigh for sigh.

II.

I 'll not leave thee thou lone one,
To pine on the stem;
Since the lovely are sleeping,
Go sleep thou with them.
Thus kindly I scatter
Thy leaves o'er the bed,
Where thy mates of the garden
Lie scentless and dead.

III.

Mar súd is dúal imṫeaċt, 'nuair a ċríonas an gráḋ,
'S 'nuair euluiġeas ó na seóidiḃ an sgéiṁ a's an bláṫ;
'Nuair a claoiḋtear na croiḋṫe, scap suarcas a's seun,
Cia ḃeiḋeaḋ, mar ċaḋan aonaraċ sa t-saoġal so leis féin.

ÓG-LAOĊ NA RANN.

Fonn—Móirín.

I.

Do ṫriall ċum caṫa óg-laoċ na rann,
  Lár náṁaid Eireann ársaiġe;
Lann aṫar fáisgṫe air go teann,
  Ann aoinḟeaċt le n-a ċláirsiġ.
A ṫír na n-dán! deir an laoċ-ċeoil grinn,
  Da m-beiḋeaḋ an saoġal do d' ḋaoraḋ,
Tá aon ċruit aṁáin le do ṁolaḋ go binn,
  'S aon lann aṁáin le do ḟaoraḋ.

II.

Do ṫuit an bárd! aċt má ṫuit, go fóill
  Ḃí a ċroiḋe neaṁ-eaglaċ, treunṁar;
A's raob se teuda cláirsiġe an ċeoil,
  Do scuab sé, an trá ḃí seunṁar:
A's dúḃairt, "Ní ṁillfiḋ cuing do ġuṫ,
  "A ċruit ċaoin na ḃ-feaṫ saora;
"Is ní cluinfear go h-eug do lán ḃinn-sruṫ,
  "Lár bruide a's bróin na tíre".

III.

So soon may *I* follow,
When friendships decay,
And from Love's shining circle
The gems drop away!
When true hearts lie wither'd,
And fond ones are flown,
Oh! who would inhabit
This bleak world alone?

THE MINSTREL BOY.

Air—*Moreen.*

I.

The Minstrel Boy to the war is gone,
In the ranks of death you 'll find him;
His father's sword he has girded on,
And his wild harp slung behind him.
"Land of Song!" said the warrior bard,
"Tho' all the world betrays thee,
"*One* sword, at least, thy rights shall guard,
"*One* faithful harp shall praise thee!"

II.

The Minstrel fell!—but the foeman's chain
Could not bring his proud soul under;
The harp he lov'd ne'er spoke again,
For he tore its cords asunder;
And said, "No chains shall sully thee,
"Thou soul of love and bravery!
"Thy songs were made for the pure and free,
"They shall never sound in slavery!"

B' aoiḃinn an gleann, ḃí romam sínte.

Fonn—Cailín deas crúḋaḋ na m-bó.

I.

B' aoiḃinn an gleann ḃí rómam sínte,
Ann ar ḟág me mo ċéile 's mo ġráḋ
Is ḃí mé le roinn a' imníḋe líonta,
D' ḟág m' aigne faoi smúid a's faoi sgáṫ.
Tóruiġ mé an leus, do ġeall m' aon-searc,
Do lasaḋ, le mo soilsiuġaḋ 'sa t-sliġe,
Aċt buḋ díoṁaoin, neaṁ-ḟéiṁaṁail mo ġeur-ḋearc.
Le linn tromaċain neulta na h-oiḋċe.

II.

Ḃí a seomra a d'ionsuiġear gan tionol,
Co uaigneaċ mar uaiṁ, aċt mo ċráḋ!
Naċ sínte sa n-uaiṁ ḃí an ḃruinneall,
'N áit culuiġṫe go náireaċ 'sa trá.
Ḃí an ċruit ċeólṁar croċtá air an m-balla,
Le a m-breugsaḋ mo ḃrón, an ḃean óg,
Aċt an láṁ, a sgeiṫ a ceól ṫríd an ṫalla,
Tá aig criṫ aig a g-coigríġeaċ faoi fóg.

III.

Ḃí am ann, a ċeile ċam, ċluaineaċ,
Dá n-déanfaiḋe an sorma buḋ lúġa,
Aig cur do leiṫ cáiliḋeaċta luaineaċ',
Léimfeaḋ lann d' ḟir a cosaint do ċlú:
Aċt anois, a ḃean na d-táir-sgeul 's na n-dánta,
Is truailliġe 's is tarcuisniġe cáil,
Beirféar leór-ċúitiúġaḋ trom ann do ċáinte,
Tré ċreaċ a's tré ċráḋ Inse-fáil.

THE SONG OF O'RUARK.

AIR—*The pretty girl milking her cow.*

I.

The valley lay smiling before me
  Where lately I left her behind;
Yet I trembled, and something hung o'er me
  That sadden'd the joy of my mind.
I look'd for the lamp which, she told me,
  Should shine when her pilgrim return'd,
But, though darkness began to enfold me,
  No lamp from the battlements burn'd.

II.

I flew to her chamber—'t was lonely,
  As if the lov'd tenant lay dead;—
Ah, would it were death, and death only,
  But no, the young false one had fled.
And there hung the lute that could soften
  My very worst pains into bliss,
While the hand that had wak'd it so often
  Now throbb'd to a proud rival's kiss.

III.

There *was* a time, falsest of women!
  When Breffni's good sword would have sought
That man, through a million of foemen,
  Who dar'd but to wrong thee *in thought!*
While now—O degenerate daughter
  Of Erin! how fall'n is thy fame!
And thro' ages of bondage and slaughter,
  Our country shall bleed for thy shame.

IV.

Ta ċeana aiṗṫi an ṁallaċt gan ḟalaċ;
 Tá na coigriġ' is ḃrúideaṁla toil,
Déanaḋ sgrios air ċríċ Fóḋla go ballaċ,
 Tá á h-úir-ġleannta dearg le fuil.
Aċt forsglaiḋ an glas-ṁeirge ann áirde,
 Bíḋeaḋ fuilteaċ go láṁ suas gaċ lann,
Tá linn-ne ceart, Eire, 's ar g-cáirde,
 An aġaiḋ eagcóir' na Sasanaċ teann.

MO ṠLÁN LIḂ! AĊT TRÁ ḂEIḊIḊ.

Fonn—Moll Rún

I.

Mo ṡlán liḃ! aċt trá ḃéiḋiḋ aig failtiúġaḋ na h-oiḋċe,
Do ḋúisgas binn-ċeolta 'gur ruaigeas measg sraoi
Na dearmadaiḋe an ċarair, ḃíḋeaḋ aig cur orra bunn
'S neaṁ-ṡuimaṁail ann gaċ brón, 'nna ṡuiḋe liḃ lé fonn.
Fillfiḋ sír gan amras a ḃrón', agus ní ḃéiḋ
De'n árd-ṁuiniġin a ḃreug é, aon leaċta 'nna ḋiaiġ,
Aċt ní silfaiḋ as a ċuiṁne, de oiḋċe no de lá,
Gur ṫóg siḃ ḋe sa n-am sin, gaċ brón agus gaċ craḋ.

II

Le linn teaċt na h-oiḋċe úd sianṡaṁla, 'nna a m-bíḋeann
Gaċ croiḋe lán de ḟeun, a's gaċ cuaċ lán de ḟíon,
Má's dorċa no lonnraċ ḃéiḋeas mo ṡiúḃal ann sa t-sliġe,
Béiḋeaḋ liḃ, a ċáirde, a n-intinn 's a g-croiḋe.
Ann ḃur n-greann a's ḃur súgaiġil béiḋ agam roinn
Agus m' aigne aig éisteaċt le ḃur g-ceoltaiḃ go binn;
Is aoiḃinn, ma ḃíḋeann aon de na flaċaiḃ lo ḟáġail,
A déirfeas, "Is truaġ gan é againn ann sa' dáil".

IV.

Already the curse is upon her,
  And strangers her valleys profane;
They come to divide—to dishonour,
  And tyrants they long will remain.
But onward!—the green banner rearing,
  Go flesh every sword to the hilt;
On *our* side is Virtue and Erin,
  On *theirs* is the Saxon and Guilt.

FAREWELL!—BUT WHENEVER YOU WELCOME THE HOUR.

AIR—*Moll Roone.*

I.

Farewell!—but whenever you welcome the hour
That awakens the night-song of mirth in your bower,
Then think of the friend who once welcom'd it too,
And forgot his own griefs to be happy with you.
His griefs may return, not a hope may remain
Of the few that have brighten'd his pathway of pain:
But he ne'er will forget the short vision that threw
Its enchantment around him, while ling'ring with you.

II.

And still on that evening, when pleasure fills up
To the highest top sparkle each heart and each cup,
Where'er my path lies, be it gloomy or bright,
My soul, happy friends, shall be with you that night;
Shall join in your revels, your sports, and your wiles,
And return to me beaming all o'er with your smiles—
Too blest if it tells me that, 'mid the gay cheer,
Some kind voice had murmur'd, "I wish he were here!"

III.

'N aiṁḋeoin gaċ dó-ḃeirt d'a n-imreann an saoġal,
Ḃiḋeann d'éis na féine, taise geal a's fuiġeall,
Do ċiḋtear lár ḃróin agus imniḋe na h-oiḋċe
'Eidiġte leis an sgeiṁ air a deáġ-ġnúis do ḃí.
Go m-buḋ buan leis an g-cuiṁne so do líonfar mo ċroiḋe,
Mar an soiṫeaċ m-biḋeann rúṫ rós d'a ṡilt ann, a's brís,
Má brisfar é 's má brúiġtaer, go n-déantar dé spréiḋ,
Béiḋ balaḋ bréaġ na rós, air gaċ roinn de'n t-soiṫeaċ cré.

A CUIṀNE LEAT EIBLÍN, SEOD 'S SGAIṪ ÓIGE.

Fonn—Da m-buḋ Cléireaċ me.

I.

A cuiṁne leat Eiblín, seod 's sgaiṫ óige
Ar m-baile, 'd' ḟan suairc agus sáiṁ faoi sgeaċ
'Nuair do ṫóruiġ Uilliam eiltreaċ mar ċéile í,
'S bí a d-teaċín faoi ċuimirc riaġaltais ġráḋ.

II.

Bí aig saoṫruġaḋ a n-aoinḟeaċt faoi ḃáisteaċ a's sian,
'Gur dubairt Uilliam sa ḋeoiġ lé duḃ-ḃrón croiḋe:
"A n-ait eile tóroġmuid táinte 'gus díon",
Gúr ṫriall sí ó' m-baile aig osnaiġeal 'sa t-sliġe.

III.

Buḋ fada 's buḋ tuirseaċ aig siúbal do bí,
'Gur aigne na h-óige le imniḋ fann;
'Nuair aig claonaḋ lae doininn, bí garb lé gaoṫ,
Súd air aṁarc, lann flaṫaṁail a lár na g-crann.

III.

Let fate do her worst, there are relics of joy,
Bright dreams of the past, which she cannot destroy;
Which come in the night-time of sorrow and care,
And bring back the features that joy used to wear.
Long, long be my heart with such memories filled!
Like the vase, in which roses have once been distill'd—
You may break, you may shatter the vase, if you will,
But the scent of the roses will hang round it still.

YOU REMEMBER ELLEN.

AIR—*Were I a clerk.*

I.

You remember Ellen, our hamlet's pride,
  How meekly she bless'd her humble lot,
When the stranger, William, had made her his bride,
  And love was the light of their lowly cot.

II.

Together they toil'd through winds and rains,
  Till William, at length, in sadness said,
"We must seek our fortune on other plains";
  Then, sighing she left her lowly shed.

III.

They roam'd a long and a weary way,
  Nor much was the maiden's heart at ease,
When now, at the close of one stormy day,
  They see a proud castle among the trees.

IV.

"Ann so", air an t-óg-ḟear "glacamuid scíṫ,
"Tá an oiḋċe mall 'gus an gaoṫ teann":
Do ḟéid se an t-aḋarc le iomċar árd-saoi,
'S d' uṁluiġ, aig dul steaċ ḋó, an doirseoir a ċeann.

V.

"D' ḟáilte, bean uasal", do ġáir an saoi,
"'S leat an ċoill a's an dún so, 's gaċ niḋ tá ann,
As báiniḋ, ṁeas bréaṫra, a raiḃ annta bríġ,
'Oir sí Eiḃlín bean tiġearna Ros na Lann.

VI.

'S air a ċéile tá síor-ċeanaṁail 's gráḋaċ an luan,
D'iarr Uilliam an t-eiltreaċ 's do ṗós mar ṁnaoi,
Sa a lár na g-crann tiġearnaṁail tá téagraċ, buan,
Mar 's an teaċín ó—ar téigeaḋ tá' ġnaoi.

do ġuilfinn muinigin ṁealltaċ.

Fonn—an cran-rósa.

I.

Do ġuilfinn muinigin ṁealltaċ,
Da d-tréigfeá-sa me, a ġráḋ;
Do ċaoinfinn carad ḟealltaċ',
Da ḃ-feallfá-sa orm 'san trá.
Aċt fad a's tá do ḃlaḋ-dearc
Aig soilsiúġaḋ air mo ṡliġe go buan,
Ní ḃeiḋ brón orm, a ċeud-searc,
Naċ g-cuirfiḋ tu go síor faoi ṡuan.

IV.

"To-night", said the youth, "we 'll shelter there;
"The wind blows cold, the hour is late":
So he blew the horn with a chieftain's air,
And the porter bow'd as they pass'd the gate.

V.

"Now, welcome, Lady!" exclaim'd the youth,
"This castle is thine, and these dark woods all!"
She believ'd him craz'd, but his words were truth,
For Ellen is Lady of Rosna Hall!

VI.

And dearly the lord of Rosna loves
What William the stranger woo'd and wed;
And the light of bliss, in these lordly groves,
Shines pure as it did in the lowly shed.

I 'D MOURN THE HOPES THAT LEAVE ME.

AIR—*The Rose tree.*

I.

I 'd mourn the hopes that leave me,
If thy smiles had left me too;
I 'd weep when friends deceive me,
If thou wert, like them, untrue.
But while I 've thee before me,
With heart so warm and eyes so bright,
No clouds can linger o'er me,
That smile turns them all to light.

II.

Ní 'l anns an t-saoġal go h-uile,
  Mo ċráḋaḋ, agus tú ḃeiṫ liom;
Tá aoiḃneas gan dile,
  'S gan ruin leat 'nna ḃuaiḋréaḋ ṫriom:
B'ḟeárr an aisling 's breugaiġe,
  'S mé smuaineaḋ ort-sa, a ṡearc mo ċroiḋe,
'Ná 'n súḃaċas 's mó, 's is aeraiġe,
  'S mé sgarṫa uait-sé le mo ḃiṫ.

III.

Giḋ gur ḟeall na gallta
  Do ċealg sinn lé cluain 's le breug
'S gur tuar ḋúinn do ḃeiṫ meallta,
  Ḃeiṫ a tnúṫ leo arís go h-eug.
Béiḋ solus ans a dúḃaċan,
  Aig treoruġaḋ m' aisdir seasda coiḋċe;
Mar tá 'n intleaċt seiġ naċ múċann,
  A's leus do smígeaḋ a ḃ-fasgaḋ ar d-tíġ.

IV.

D'éis an t-solus a ḃeiṫ múċta,
  Do ṫreoruiġ é ṫríd an t-sliġe,
Tig eagla air ḟear siúḃalta
  Aig sorruġaḋ bealaiġ lár na h-oiḋċe.
Aċt fós le lóċrann reulta
  Is lonnraċ, seasṁaċ seasda a siúḃal,
'Oir ní 'l leus aig déalraḋ neulta,
  Mar an leus a ṫig ó ríġ na n-dúl.

II.

'T is not in fate to harm me,
  While fate leaves thy love to me;
'T is not in joy to charm me,
  Unless joy be shared with thee.
One minute's dream about thee,
  Were worth a long, an endless year
Of waking bliss without thee,
  My own love, my only dear;

III.

And tho' the hope be gone, love,
  That long sparkled o'er our way,
Oh! we shall journey on, love,
  More safely without its ray.
Far better lights shall win me
  Along the path I 've yet to roam—
The mind that burns within me,
  And pure smiles from thee at home.

IV.

Thus, when the lamp that lighted
  The traveller at first, goes out,
He feels awhile benighted,
  And looks around in fear and doubt.
But soon, the prospect clearing,
  By cloudless starlight on he treads,
And thinks no lamp so cheering
  As that light which Heaven sheds.

Ḃ-fuil d' óg-laete seunṁar faoi lionn-duḃ?

Fonn— Patruic Cluaineaċ.

I.

Ḃ-fuil d' óg-laete seunṁar' faoi lionn-duḃ,
  Mar ṁaidin faoi slam de 'n ċeó?
'S ro luaṫ do ċuaiḋ ṫarainn-ne teann-sruṫ
  An am', nár ġnáṫaċ brón gan sóġ
Ḃ-fuil sionta na h-aoise geur', cruaiḋe,
  Teaċt air ċroiḋe a ḃí aerac go leór?
Tar ċugam, a leinḃ na truaiġe,
  A's silfead leat deor le deor.

II.

An aṁail le ċre Ċil-ṁiontain
  An gean air ar ċlaon do ċroiḋe,
A m-biḋeann cruṫre trí sléiḃte is gleanntáin
  Aig dealraḋ ann gaċ áit d'ar sliġe?
Aċt d' eis mórán saoṫair aig róṁar
  Na cré, 'nn a ḃ-fuil ór féin cáil',
Tá ar saoṫar gan toraḋ, gan sóġṁar,
  Gan aon niḋ 'nna ḋiaiġ le fáġail.

III.

Raiḃ do ḋóiġ, mar cun na soir-rioġaċt'
  Dul ó ċrann go cran, deir an sgeul,
Aig taisbeanaḋ seoide na draoiḋeaċt'
  Ḃí soilseaċ le glóir, ó n-a ḃeul?
Air ċraoḃ d' eis craoiḃe aig seasaḋ,
  Súd ċugad a seoid air a n-geug,
Aċt d' eis tú a ṁeallaḋ, le casaḋ,
  Súd uait sí arís go h-eug.

HAS SORROW THY YOUNG DAYS SHADED?

AIR—*Sly Patrick.*

I

Has sorrow thy young days shaded,
As clouds o'er the morning fleet?
Too fast have those young days faded,
That, even in sorrow, were sweet?
Does Time with his cold wing wither
Each feeling that once was dear?—
Then, child of misfortune, come hither,
I 'll weep with thee tear for tear.

II.

Has love to that soul, so tender,
Been like our Lagenian mine,
Where sparkles of golden splendour
All over the surface shine?
But, if in pursuit we go deeper,
Allur'd by the gleam that shone,
Ah! false as the dream of the sleeper,
Like Love, the bright ore is gone.

III.

Has Hope, like the bird in the story,
That flitted from tree to tree
With the talisman's glittering glory—
Has Hope been that bird to thee?
On branch after branch alighting,
The gem did she still display,
And, when nearest and most inviting,
Then waft the fair gem away?

IV.

Má euluiġ mar súd am na milse,
  Nár ḟearḃuiġ aon lá d' ar m-biṫ;
Má 's meallṫaċ fríṫ muinġin na dilse
  A lonnruiġ duḃ-neulta ar g-croiḋe:
Má 's críonta mar súd le gaeṫiḃ cruaiḋe
  Tá gaċ cáiliḋeaċt ḃí gráḋaċ go leor:
Tar ċugam, a leinḃ na truaiġe,
  A's silfead leat deor le deor.

NÍ RAIḂ ĊO FAILTEAṀAIL.

Fonn—Lag an Laġa.

I.

Ní raiḃ ċo failteaṁail na ceolta síġe
  Teaċt air neaċ suanṁar go fóill a riaṁ,
Tre leiṫ-duisġṫe as táṁ na h-oiḋċe,
  Cluinneas feaċ' neaṁḋa binn' le n-a ṫaoḃ—
Do ḃris sár-ġuṫ orm 'san am raiḃ baiṫte,
  An croiḋe 'n mo lár faoi ṫrom-ṡlam ceo,
Gan doiġ go cluinfaiḋ ċoiḋċe an deoraiḋe cráiḋte,
  Fonn ċo binn beannuiġṫe, arus go deo.

II.

Guṫ binn na dilse, mar ċiun-gaoṫ samraiḋ,
  Go sáiṁ aig éaluġaḋ triḋ duala cam',
A's casta sligeáin, ḃí fuaim na h-aṁara,
  'Teaċt triḋ gaċ cuas de mo ċroiḋe 'san am.
Buḋ íc a g-cogar é, buḋ lóċrann grianṁar
  'Ga luaḋ; a's b' ḟeárr liom 'na an saoġal gan roinn
Mo ṫrom-ṫáṁ fada, tá le duḃ-ḃrón lionṁar,
  Beiṫ brisṫe aig ceoltaiḃ ċo beannuiġṫe binn.

IV.

If thus the young hours have fleeted,
  When sorrow itself look'd bright;
If thus the fair hope hath cheated,
  That led thee along so light;
If thus the cold world now wither
  Each feeling that once was dear:—
Come, child of misfortune, come hither,
  I 'll weep with thee, tear for tear.

NO, NOT MORE WELCOME.

AIR—*Luggelaw.*

I.

No, not more welcome the fairy numbers
  Of music fall on the sleeper's ear,
When, half awaking from fearful slumbers,
  He thinks the full choir of heaven is near—
Then came that voice, when, all forsaken,
  This heart long had sleeping lain,
Nor thought its cold pulse would ever waken
  To such benign, blessed sounds again.

II.

Sweet voice of comfort! 't was like the stealing
  Of summer wind thro' some wreathèd shell—
Each secret winding, each inmost feeling
  Of all my soul echo'd to its spell!—
'T was whisper'd balm—'t was sunshine spoken!—
  I 'd live years of grief and pain
To have my long sleep of sorrow broken
  By such benign, blessed sounds again.

AIG TÚS AR G-CAIDREAḊ.

Fonn—A Ṗatruic teiċ uaim.

I.

Aig tus ar g-caidreaḋ 's tú óg-ḃláṫ
  Ḃíḋis ċo fial a n-gealltaiḃ,
Ar ċosṁail dúiḃ ḃeiṫ fíor gan sċáṫ,
  Nár smuaineas do ḃeiṫ meallta.
N'eis tú ḃeiṫ aṫruiġṫe, d' ḟan síor-ḃeo,
  Mo ṁuinniġin asat gan faonaḋ,
Da ḃ-feallfáḋ air an t-saoġal go deo,
  Uaim féin naċ n-déanfá claonaḋ;
    Aċt imṫiġ leat, ḟir ċaim na m-breug,
      Is cóir an croiḋe ḃeiṫ briste,
    Do ċuirfeaḋ dóiġ arís go h-eug
      A g-cluanaire ċo cliste.

II.

Trá ḃi gaċ beul aig luaḋ do ḃaois,
  B' olc liom an sgeul duḃ gráineaṁail,
Nó, ṫargair mé go sgeiṫfeaḋ aois,
  Glóir, as an óige ċáineaṁail.
Duit ḃi seasṁaċ, buan mo ġráḋ,
  'Nuair ḃi do ċáirde glonnṁar,
'S an croiḋe tá le do ċluain' craḋ
  A ḟuil ḋoirtfeaḋ duit go fonṁar.
    Aċt imṫiġ leat, ḟir ċluanaiġ, ċaim,
      'S ó an t-séis a ḃ-fuilir ḃáiṫte,
    Aig dúsaċt, tuigfir ann's an am
      Geur aṁgar croiḋṫe craiḋte.

WHEN FIRST I MET THEE.

AIR—*O Patrick, fly from me.*

I.

When first I met thee, warm and young,
  There shone such truth about thee,
And on thy lip such promise hung,
  I did not dare to doubt thee.
I saw thee change, yet still relied,
  Still clung with hope the fonder,
And thought, tho' false to all beside,
  From me thou couldst not wander.
    But go, deceiver! go—
      The heart, whose hopes could make it
    Trust one so false, so low,
      Deserves that thou shouldst break it.

II.

When every tongue thy follies nam'd,
  I fled th' unwelcome story;
Or found, in ev'n the faults they blam'd,
  Some gleams of future glory.
I still was true, when nearer friends
  Conspir'd to wrong, to slight thee:
The heart, that now thy falsehood rends,
  Would then have bled to right thee.
    But go, deceiver! go—
      Some day, perhaps thou 'lt waken
    From pleasure's dream, to know
      The grief of hearts forsaken.

Ní feicṫear leus na h-aois' sa tra
  Ḃ-fuil aig bláṫ na h-oige tréigṫe,
Ṫeiṫ an dream, aig a raiḃ ort gráḋ,
  'S ta ort gráin ó luċt do ḃreugṫa.
Measg tráill, tá fleaḋ antráṫaċ na h-oiḋċe
  'Ga roinn gan téagar saoiḋeaṁail,
'S mar leus air uaiṁ, ḃ-fuil bás ann faoi,
  Tá 'smuige fuar neaṁ-ċroiḋeaṁail.
    Imṫiġ: 's da m-beiḋeaḋ air do laiṁ,
      'Or a's táinte an domain,
    Ní ṫiuḃrainn deor de ġol ġlan sáiṁ,
      Air do saiḃreas olc, mar róġain.

IV.

'S b' féidir go d-tiocfaḋ, 'ċluanaiġ, an lá,
  'M-béiḋ na cuinge so féin 'ga m-briseaḋ,
A m-béiḋir aig blaoḋaċ gan féiḋm le cráḋ,
  Air an té ḃeiḋeas ort aig cliseaḋ.
Té ḃeirfeaḋ duit-se fuil a croiḋe,
  Trá, ḃeiḋ sagṫa leunmar,
Aig taisbeaint duit gur ṫuill tú an gnaoi
  Ḃi aici ort 's tú seunmar,
    Uaim, uaim! mallaċt duit ni fiú,
      D' imḋeargaḋ 's níḋ craiḋṫe,
    Fuaṫ féin ni aṫċuingoċaḋ duit mí-ċliu
      Ċo trom a's táir ann báiṫte.

III.

Even now, tho' youth its bloom has shed,
  No lights of age adorn thee:
The few, who lov'd thee once, have fled,
  And they who flatter scorn thee.
Thy midnight cup is pledg'd to slaves,
  No genial ties enwreath it;
The smiling there, like light on graves,
  Has rank cold hearts beneath it.
    Go—go—tho' worlds were thine,
      I would not now surrender
    One taintless tear of mine
      For all thy guilty splendour!

IV.

And days may come, thou false one! yet,
  When even those ties shall sever;
When thou wilt call with vain regret
  On her thou 'st lost for ever,—
On her who, in thy fortune's fall,
  With smiles had still received thee,
And gladly died to prove thee all
  Her fancy first believed thee.
    Go—go—'t is vain to curse,
      'T is weakness to upbraid thee:
    Hate cannot wish thee worse,
      Than guilt and shame have made thee.

ĊO ḞAD A'S ḂI CEOLRAIḊ.

Fonn—Paddi Fair.

I.

Ċo ḟad a's ḃí ceolraiḋ na h-eaċtra aig cúṁdaċ go h-aireaċ,
Gaċ niḋ d'a raiḃ fiġte 'n duḃ-eige na sníṫ,
Le n'a ṫaoḃ ḃí Neaċ Eireann go brónaċ 's go faireaċ.
'Oir an stáir smalaḋ leaḃra d' a cuid-san do ḃí
Aċt o! mar do las suas a rosc ċrud an g-ceo,
Trá n' éis iomad bliaḋanta de ḋuḃ-ḃrón gan scíṫ,
Ḋearc an ċeolraiḋ go beo,
Le sgrioḃ' ḋealruiġ go deo,
Gaċ duilleóg, aig cuir síos tír-ḟlaṫ, car a croiḋe.

II.

Failte! realt ġéal na Banba. air an Neaċ a's í faluiġṫe,
Faoi ġaeṫ' ṫig ó sséir drúċdaṁail Eireann le glóir,
Trí bliaḋanta de ċraḋ a's ó cara mé dealuiġṫe,
Ḃiḋeas air crúiġ ṁóir lóċrain mar ṫusa, cur tóir.
Ciḋ mór minir laoċra beiṫ 'ga luaḋ air mo ṫaoḃ,
Air cam-ċasáin iompáiḋ, faraor! tá n'a luiḋe
Aċt tá 'gur ḃí riaṁ,
Gan aon smal an craoḃ,
Tá timċioll air ċeann ḃuaḋaċ ċaraid mo ċroiḋe.

III.

Aċt roṁat tá an saoṫar is mó ann do ḃeaṫa.
A ḃéirsfeas air a n-dearnais a riaṁ go fóill bárr
Ciḋ buḋ céimeaṁail ḃeiṫ saoraḋ críċe eile a g-caṫa,
Is mó an réim, do ṫír féin a tógḃail, tá 'r lár,
Toig aig caṫaoir na ríġṫe do ċosnais, do ġuṫ,
'Gur agair air son Eireann, 'd' oil ard-tuaṫ do ḃiṫ,
S' air áṁan buairṫe ḋuḃ;
D'a fuil 's deora, sruṫ,
Mar ṫuaġ-ċeaṫa doiġe, biḋeaḋ an laoċ, car a croiḋe.

WHILE HISTORY'S MUSE.

AIR—*Paddy Whack.*

I.

While History's Muse the memorial was keeping
  Of all that the dark hand of Destiny weaves,
Beside her the Genius of Erin stood weeping,
  For hers was the story that blotted the leaves.
But oh! how the tear in her eyelids grew bright,
When, after whole pages of sorrow and shame,
    She saw History write,
    With a pencil of light,
That illumin'd the whole volume, her Wellington's name.

II.

"Hail, Star of my Isle!" said the Spirit, all sparkling
  With beams such as break from her own dewy skies—
"Thro' ages of sorrow, deserted and darkling,
  "I 've watch'd for some glory like thine to arise.
"For tho' heroes I 've number'd, unblest was their lot,
"And unhallow'd they sleep in the cross-ways of Fame:—
    "But oh! there is not
    "One dishonouring blot
"On the wreath that encircles my Wellington's name!

III.

"Yet still the last crown of thy toils is remaining,
  "The grandest, the purest, even *thou* hast yet known;
"Tho' proud was thy task, other nations unchaining,
  "Far prouder to heal the deep wounds of thy own.
"At the foot of that throne for whose weal thou hast stood,
  "Go plead for the land that first cradled thy fame—
    "And bright o'er the flood
    "Of her tears and her blood;
"Let the rainbow of Hope be her Wellington's name!"

TRIḊ ḂRÓN 'GUS TRIḊ GAḂAḊ.

Fonn—Uair ḃí agam fíor-ġráḋ.

I.

Triḋ brón 'gus triḋ ġábaḋ, do loinriġ do smuigeaḋ mo ṡliġe,
Gur sgeiṫ doiġ air gaċ dreisóg, mo ṫimċiol ḃí 'nna luiḋe:
D'a duiḃe crann ar m-beaṫa, buḋ soilseaċ ḃí ar n-gráḋ,
Go raiḃ glóir ann áit náire, 'gus caon-dúraċt ann áit sgáṫ.
O! sgláḃ gíḋ do raiḃ me, ann d' uċtse saor do ḃí,
'S ṫug beannaċt do 'n doilġis do ṁeuduiġ dom gean do ċroiḋe.

II.

Ḃí do ċoṁṡuirriġeaċ faoi urram 'gus tu faoi ḋímeas mór,
Ḃí do ċróin-se de deilg, 's a cróin-san de ór.
'Suiriġ sí-se an teampal; 's tu-sa n-guais na n-gleann,
Buḋ oirc ṡiad a caraid 's do daraid-se 'nna sclaḃ' san'.
Aċt b' ḟearr liom 'san uaiṁ aig do ċosaiḃ ḃeiṫ mo luiḋe,
'Na ḃeiṫ pórsa le rud fuaṫṁar, no aig iompuġaḋ uait mo ċroiḋe.

III.

Cia deir gur fann do ġeallta, beir ort breiṫe cruaiḋ;
Da m-beiḋeaḋ fealltaċ, ní gan lasaḋ ḃeiḋeaḋ do ġruaiḋ,
Deirtear, ort ċo fad ḃí fáisgṫe cuiḃre trom',
Go b-fuil do ċroiḋe le sclaḃaċt clóite 'gus tu crom:
O! na creid ṡiad, níor b' ḟeidir le cuing ṫu do ċlaoiḋ.
'N áit a soilsiġeann do spiorad, soilsiġeann saorsa ċoiḋċe.

THE IRISH PEASANT TO HIS MISTRESS

AIR—*I once had a true love.*

I.

Through grief and through danger thy smile hath cheer'd my way,
Till hope seem'd to bud from each thorn that round me lay;
The darker our fortune, the brighter our pure love burn'd,
Till shame into glory, till fear into zeal was turn'd;
Yes, slave as I was, in thy arms my spirit felt free,
And blessed even the sorrows that made me more dear to thee.

II.

Thy rival was honour'd whilst thou wert wrong'd and scorn'd,
Thy crown was of briers, while gold her brows adorn'd;
She woo'd me to temples, while thou layest hid in caves,
Her friends were all masters, while thine, alas! were slaves;
Yet cold in the earth, at thy feet, I would rather be,
Than wed what I love not, or turn one thought from thee.

III.

They slander thee sorely, who say thy vows are frail—
Hadst thou been a false one, thy cheek had look'd less pale!
They say too, so long thou hast worn those lingering chains,
That deep in thy heart they have printed thy servile stains.
Oh! foul is the slander! no chain could that soul subdue.
Where shineth *thy* spirit, there liberty shineth too.

IS FAD ṠI O'N G-CRÍĊ.

Fonn—Fosgail an doras.

I.

Is fad ṡi o'n g-críċ, ḃ-fuil a h-óg-laoċ 'nn a luiḋe
'S gan aird air a suirġiḃ 'g a ḃreugaḋ;
Aċt iompiġeann go fuar ó ṡúiliḃ gaċ saoi,
'Oir tá a croiḋe le n-a ceile 'g a cugaḋ.

II.

Buḋ ṡiad aḃráin duṫċais á tír' féin do ṡeinn,
Rinn gaċ fearsa d' ar áil leis do ṁeaṁaraḋ.
O 's beag imniḋe loċt cluinste a ceolta binn;
A croiḋe ḃeiṫ 'g a ḃriseaḋ gan caḃaraḋ.

III.

Do ṁair se d' a rún; agus d'eug se d'a ċríċ:
So an meud ḃí 'ga ċeangail air talaṁ:
Ní luaṫ 'ġaḃfas trom-ġul a ṫíre aon sgiṫ,
'S ní ḃeiḋ 'ḃ-fad gan a ċéile an uaiṁ fálaṁ.

IV.

O déann uaiṁ di 's an áit ḃ-fuil na gaeṫ' gréine 'siar,
'Nuair ġealleann siad máraċ glóraċ:
Beiḋ 'soilsuġaḋ air a suan mar smigeaḋ ann iar
'O n-a dil-innis féin a tá ḃrónaċ.

SHE IS FAR FROM THE LAND.

AIR—*Open the door.*

I.

She is far from the land where her young hero sleeps,
And lovers are round her sighing;
But coldly she turns from their gaze, and weeps,
For her heart in his grave is lying.

II.

She sings the wild songs of her dear native plains,
Every note which he lov'd awaking;—
Ah! little they think who delight in her strains,
How the heart of the Minstrel is breaking.

III.

He had liv'd for his love, for his country he died:
They were all that to life had entwin'd him:
Nor soon shall the tears of his country be dried,
Nor long will his love stay behind him.

IV.

Oh! make her a grave where the sunbeams rest
When they promise a glorious morrow:
They 'll shine o'er her sleep like a smile from the West,
From her own lov'd island of sorrow.

CA Ḃ-FUIL AN TRAIL IS TAIRE.

Fonn—Sios agus síos liom.

I.

Ca ḃ-fuil an tráil is táire
A ngéibeal cruaiḋ, tuar náire,
    Dá m-beiḋeaḋ ann,
    Nać d-tairnóćaḋ lann
'N áit meaṫ' faoi ċuing gan gáire?
Cia an croiḋe faoi éigceart claonta,
A d-fanfaḋ lé ḃeiṫ aonta:
    'S go m-b' aoiḃin dó,
    Da m-beiḋeaḋ síor-ḃeo
Ann uċt an áird-ríġ, sínte.
Slán leat, Eire!—biḋ slán,
A ċaoimeas ar n-ár le deoraiḃ lán.

II.

Ní annsa an laiḃreal fásaḋ
Tá beo gan baint, gan básuġaḋ,
    'Na an dlaoiġ gan bláṫ,
    A ġníḋ fleasg a's sgáṫ
Do'n m-buaḋaċ, buḋ dual a sásúġaḋ.
Tá ar g-cos air úr ar g-cairde;
Tá an glas-meirg' tógṫa ann áirde;
    'S iad lé n-ar d-taoḃ,
    Nár ċlis a riaṁ,
'S an náṁaid romainn 's os aird.
Slán leat, Eire! biḋ slán,
A ċaoimeas ar n-ár le deoraiḃ lán.

OH! WHERE 'S THE SLAVE.

AIR—*Sios aguś sios lom.*

I.

Oh! where 's the slave so lowly,
Condemn'd to chains unholy,
Who, could he burst
His bonds at first,
Would pine beneath them slowly?
What soul, whose wrongs degrade it,
Would wait till time decay'd it,
When thus its wing
At once may spring
To the throne of him who made it?
Farewell, Erin,—farewell, all
Who live to weep our fall.

II.

Less dear the laurel growing
Alive, untouch'd, and blowing,
Than that whose braid
Is pluck'd to shade
The brows with victory glowing.
We tread the land that bore us,
Her green flag glitters o'er us,
The friends we 've tried
Are by our side,
And the foe we hate before us.
Farewell, Erin—farewell, all
Who live to weep our fall.

AIR M' UĊT FÉIN GLAC SUAN.

Fonn—Loċ Silin.

I.

Mo ḋíl eilit loite! air m' uċt féin glac suan:
Giḋ gur ċuluiġ an treud uait, so d' áit dídin buan,
Tá an smígeaḋ ann gan dúḃċan, 'gus searc-ċuman croiḋe,
Gus láṁ le do ċosaint le congial, gan sgíṫ.

II.

An teas-ġráḋ, go marraḋ se seasṁaċ, naċ cóir,
Tre ḃrón á's tre ġáirdeas, tre náire 's tre glóir,
Ní 'lim colgaċ no muiniḋeaċ, má táir air ċoire saor,
Aċt tá's a'm, cia ḃiḋ tú, go ḃ-fuil mo ġráḋ ort-sa fíor.

III.

Do ġáir orm aingeal, trá ḃí tú a seun,
Beiḋ me mar aingeal, trá ṫu ḃeiṫ faoi leun;
Aig lean'ṁuint do lorg, tre ġeur-ṫeinte teo,
Go do ċosaint 's do ċúṁdaċt, le mo ḃás no mo ḃeo.

COME, REST IN THIS BOSOM.

AIR—*Lough Sheeling.*

I.

Come, rest in this bosom, my own stricken deer,
Tho' the herd have fled from thee, thy home is still here;
Here still is the smile that no cloud can o'ercast,
And a heart and a hand all thy own to the last.

II.

Oh! what was love made for, if 't is not the same
Thro' joy and thro' torment, thro' glory and shame?
I know not, I ask not, if guilt 's in that heart,
I but know that I love thee whatever thou art.

III.

Thou hast call'd me thy Angel in moments of bliss,
And thy Angel I 'll be 'mid the horrors of this,
Thro' the furnace, unshrinking, thy steps to pursue,
And shield thee, and save thee, or perish there too.

TÁ EULUIĠṪE GO DEÓ UAINN AN LÓĊRANN BÍ A SGARAḊ.

Fonn—S'a ṁuirnín dílis.

I.

Tá euluiġṫe go deó uainn an lóċrann bí a sgaraḋ
  Mar ḋealraḋ an lae ġil aig soillsiuġaḋ gaċ ball:
Aig beoḋaċan le n-a ġaeṫiḃ uaiṁe na mairḃ,
  'S a líonaḋ le n-a ṡolus na súile bí dall.
Tá euluiġṫe—'s an lonnair, a d' ḟág se mar reulta,
Ní ġníḋ aċt glan-leursgus do ṫabairt air na neulta,
Ḃéiḋear aig dúban air rıġaċtaiḃ an doṁan air feaḋ saoġalta,
  Aċt go h-áirḋe ort, Eirinn! a ċuisle mo ċroiḋe.

II.

'Oir b' árd bí do ḋóiġ, trá bí an ġlóir úd d'a soillsiúġaḋ
  Do ṫimċioll trí neulta triom', dorċa an t-saoġail:
'Oir bí sinne n'eis a geur-ċuing do ḃriseaḋ, aig soillsiúġaḋ
  'Nuair aṁail mar ġaċ gréine, a briaṫa do sgaoil.
O! ní ċiḋféar ċoiḋċe arís, annsa g-cruinne
Aon am ċo h-aoiḃin, óir bí caoiṁ-ġuṫ gaċ cinne
'S gaċ rıġaċt' aig cur le ċéile: 's b' árd, binn do cluinneaḋ
  Maidin-ċeol na saoirse, seinn Eire ó ċroiḋe.

III.

Aċt gráine air na tíoráin, nár b' áil leo aċt daoirsaċt,
  'S air an táir-dream, nár ċlaon le n-a maiṫ féin a d-toil,
Bí aig caiḋreaḋ, mar andrais, óig-ḋóiġ na saoirsaċt',
  'S aig altóir na h-aise do ḃaird í le fuil.
D' euluiġ go deo uainn an aisling ḃreáġ ġrianṁar,
Ḃeiḋear d' aiṁḋeoin na g-croiḋṫe sonaṁadaċ neaṁ-ċlaonṁar,
Mar d'éiriġ ó ṫus ort go lonnraċ, 's go líonṁar,
  Eire, 'tír ċaillte, tír tairse mo ċroiḋe.

'T IS GONE, AND FOR EVER.

AIR—'*Sa mhuirnin dilis.*

I.

'T is gone, and for ever, the light we saw breaking,
  Like Heaven's first dawn o'er the sleep of the dead—
When Man, from the slumber of ages awaking,
  Look'd upward, and bless'd the pure ray, ere it fled.
'T is gone, and the gleams it has left of its burning
But deepen the long night of bondage and mourning,
That dark o'er the kingdoms of earth is returning,
  And darkest of all, hapless Erin, o'er thee.

II.

For high was thy hope, when those glories were darting
  Around thee thro' all the gross clouds of the world;
When Truth, from her fetters indignantly starting,
  At once like a Sun-burst her banner unfurled.
Oh! never shall earth see a moment so splendid—
Then, then—had one Hymn of Deliverance blended
The tongues of all nations—how sweet had ascended
  The first note of Liberty, Erin, from thee!

III.

But, shame on those tyrants who envied the blessing!
  And shame on the light race unworthy its good,
Who, at Death's reeking altar, like Furies caressing
  The young hope of Freedom, baptiz'd it in blood!
Then vanish'd for ever that bright, sunny vision,
Which, spite of the slavish, the cold heart's derision,
Shall long be remember'd, pure, bright, and elysian,
  As first it arose, my lost Erin, on thee.

DO ĊONNAIRC AIR MAIDIN.

Fonn—Moll.

I.

Do ċonnairc air maidin, air an ṁuir d'éis a líonta,
  An long breáġ faoi ḟeoltaiḃ go h-álum aig snáṁ:
Do ḋearcas arís,—a's an ġrian tar éis claonta—
  Ḃí an long air an gaineaṁ, 's an tuile 'néis tráġaḋ.

II.

Súd sompla air ṁuinín a's air ṁearḃall na baoise,
  Mar súd culuiġeas laeṫe ar sláinte 's ar réim.
Ḃíḋeann na tonna, air ar rinnceaḋ, d' ar d-tréigsin, teaċt aoise,
  'S d'ar b-fáġáil tráṫ-nóna air an tráiġ bán linn féin.

III.

Ná tráċt liom air ċéim, nó air ċeannas aig soilsuġaḋ
  Glean dorċa ar n-oiḋċe, már ḟáṁ-solus ré,
Aċt tabair dam gaeṫe úra na maidne aig soilsiuġaḋ
  An dúbain níos áille, 'na lóċrann luiḋe lae.

IV.

Cia ar naċ m-beiḋeaḋ cúṁa n-diaiġ am úd na dile,
  Raiḃ súbailce an ċumainn 'cur bláṫ ar a bár;
'S ċroiḋe mar ċrann, úr, álunn coille faoi ḃile,
  Sgeiṫ d'a ḋóiġ' deáġ-ḃalaḋ ó'n t-súġ ċrí n-a lár.

I SAW FROM THE BEACH

AIR—*Miss Molly.*

I.

I saw from the beach, when the morning was shining,
  A bark o'er the waters move gloriously on;
I came when the sun o'er that beach was declining,
  The bark was still there, but the waters were gone.

II.

And such is the fate of our life's early promise,
  So passing the spring-tide of joy we have known;
Each wave, that we danc'd on at morning, ebbs from us,
  And leaves us, at eve, on the bleak shore alone.

III.

Ne'er tell me of glories serenely adorning
  The close of our day, the calm eve of our night:—
Give me back, give me back the wild freshness of Morning,
  Her clouds and her tears are worth Evening's best light.

IV.

Oh! who would not welcome that moment's returning
  When passion first wak'd a new life through his frame,
And his soul—like the wood that grows precious in burning—
  Gave out all its sweets to love's exquisite flame?

AN CUAĊ MAR 'S CÓIR SUAS LÍON

Fonn—Bob a's Seon.

I

An cuaċ mar 's cóir suas líon,
  Le lin sgala doiṁin'
Silt air ṁalaiḋ braon,
  Bíḋeann ó gaċ imniḋ sleaṁain.
Ní sgaoilteár gaeṫe geur'
  An ġrinn ċo luaṫ 's ċo bríġṁar,
Le 'nuair do ṫig mar ċaor,
  Trí cuaċa lasta líonṁar.
An cuaċ, mar 's cóir suas líon
  Le lin sgala doiṁin
Silt air ṁalaiḋ braon,
  Bíḋeann ó gaċ imniḋ sleaṁain.

II.

Gabann mar deir an sgeul,
  Eigse stuama air sciaṫa
An ċaoir, 's o neaṁ na reul,
  Beir a nuas a ġaeṫe.
Mar súd 'sa b-sleaḋ ċruinn'
  Tarraingmuid go cinte,
O neaṁ na h-eágna 's grinn,
  Na gaeṫe 's geire 's tinte.
An cuaċ mar 's cóir, suas líon.

III.

Cia an bár uġdar a bí
  'S dual sior faġail ní h-iongnaḋ,
Go m-bíḋeann go sior an croiḋe
  Cum snoraid fíona claonaḋ:

FILL THE BUMPER FAIR.

AIR—*Bob and Joan.*

I.

Fill the bumper fair!
  Every drop we sprinkle
O'er the brow of Care.
  Smooths away a wrinkle.
Wit's electric flame
  Ne'er so swiftly passes,
As when thro' the frame
  It shoots from brimming glasses.
Fill the bumper fair!
  Every drop we sprinkle
O'er the brow of Care,
  Smooths away a wrinkle.

II.

Sages can, they say,
  Grasp the lightning's pinions,
And bring down its ray
  From the starr'd dominions.
So we, Sages, sit
  And 'mid bumpers bright'ning,
From the heaven of Wit
  Draw down all its lightning.

III.

Wouldst thou know what first
  Made our souls inherit
This ennobling thirst
  For wine's celestial spirit?

Do ṫárla ann an trá,
'Nuair suas go flaiṫeas d' euluiġ
An te' ġoid as, faoi sgáṫ,
An teine, reir na sgeulaiḋ
An ċuaċ mar 's cóir suas líon.

IV.

Do'n óglaċ trioll 'sa t-sliġe,
Ḃí gan soiġteaċ, gan corn,
Le tabairt 'nuas as crúċ
Na n-deaṫe geal, an gorn.
Aċt ó mar léim a ċroiḋe,
'Oir dearcaḋ measg na reulta,
Ċonairc ċuaċ 'nna luiḋe,
Ḃuḋ le Ḃaċċas subaċ na neulta,
An cuaċ mar 's cóir suas líon.

V.

Ḃí ann sa sgála braon,
'Fágaḋ n'éis na h-oiḋċe,
Ṫuit drictle annsa b-fíon,
Fuiġeall fleaḋ na saoiṫe.
Súd e rocair briġ
Fíona, air aigne flaṫa,
Súd mar ṫoigeann croiḋe
D'a d-tig as ċuaċ dé, ceaṫa.
An cuac mar 's cóir suas líon.

It chanced upon that day,
  When, as bards inform us,
Prometheus stole away
  The living fires that warm us.

IV.

The careless Youth, when up
  To Glory's fount aspiring,
Took nor urn nor cup
  To hide the pilfered fire in.
But, oh! his joy! when, round
  The halls of heaven spying,
Among the stars he found
  A bowl of Bacchus lying.

V.

Some drops were in that bowl,
  Remains of last night's pleasure,
With which the Sparks of Soul
  Mix'd their burning treasure.
Hence the goblet's shower
  Hath such spells to win us;
Hence its mighty power
  O'er that flame within us.
Fill the bumper fair!
  Every drop we sprinkle
O'er the brow of Care,
  Smooths away a wrinkle.

'CRUIT ANSA MO ṪÍRE.

Fonn—Langoli.

I.

'Ċruit ansa mo ṫíre, ann dorċadas ḃí sínte,
  Ḃí suar-ċuing na tosda ort fáisgṫe go teann;
Do ṫóig mé as geiḃeal, d' éis do ċuiḃreaċ ḃeiṫ sgaoilte,
  Air do ṫeudaiḃ sgeiṫ gaeṫe, a's solus saor-riann.
Ḃí fuaim sundaċ seaṫa do b' aeraiġe 's buḋ ḃinne,
  Aig dúsaċt do ṫeuda, 'ḃí suanṁar, ċum ceoil;
Aċt ḃíḋis ċo neaṁ-cúlgaċ air suaircas 's air luinne
  Go m-brisceann an brón trí do súgaiġil go fóill.

II.

Slán agus beannaċt le do ḃinn-gaċṫiḃ, 'ċruit ċroim,
  So an dlaoiġ déiġionaċ dánta, do déanfam' a ḋealḃ,
Téiḋ, a's codail faoi sgáil lonnraiġ gáirṫe air do suan trom,
  Go ḃ-fáġaid meura níos stuama air do ṫeudaiḃ ċiun', sealḃ.
Má ḃí croiḋe gaisgiġ treunṁair, tír-gráḋaiġ, nó suairc-saoi,
  'Ga g-corruġaḋ, aig cisdeaċt lé seinnim ar n-dann,
Ní raiḃ annam-sa aċt oiteóg neaṁ-ḃríġṁar na luaṫ-gaoiṫ',
  Agus uait-se do ṫáinic an fuaim binn aṁáin.

DEAR HARP OF MY COUNTRY.

AIR—*Langolee.*

I.

Dear Harp of my Country! in darkness I found thee,
  The cold chain of silence had hung o'er thee long,
When proudly, my own Island Harp, I unbound thee,
  And gave all thy chords to light, freedom, and song!
The warm lay of love and the light note of gladness
  Have waken'd thy fondest, thy liveliest thrill;
But so oft hast thou echo'd the deep sigh of sadness,
  That ev'n in thy mirth it will steal from thee still.

II.

Dear Harp of my Country! farewell to thy numbers:
  This sweet wreath of song is the last we shall twine;
Go, sleep with the sunshine of Fame on thy slumbers,
  Till touch'd by some hand less unworthy than mine:
If the pulse of the patriot, soldier, or lover,
  Have throbb'd at our lay, 't is thy glory alone:
I was *but* as the wind, passing heedlessly over,
  And all the wild sweetness I wak'd was thy own.

A ĊRUIT ĊAOIN.

Fonn—Caoineaḋ.

I.

A ċruit ċaoin! dúisġaim aris binn-ġaeṫe
  Do ċeoil, ḃí ḃáiṫte faoi ċodlaḋ trom:
Lár deor do sgaramar, 's arís d'éis laeṫe
  Tá do ċasaḋ a lár deor liom—
Nior ḃris ort súgraḋ, aċt mar na cláirsiġ,
  Aig a raiḃ ó neaṁ a rinn 's a stuaim,
'S do ċanaḋ bruid, mar do ḃruid go h-árraiḋ—
    Táir air na saileog' go fóill gan Fuaim.

II.

Gió, ó do ṡeinn duinn do ṫeuda ceolṁar',
  Ḃí am caiṫréime, a's n-éis cogaiḋ síoṫ,
A's b' iomḋa croiḋe, do léim le dóṫċus glóṙṁar
  Tá anois faoi náire duḃ, trom, 'nn a luiḋe—
Aċt ċó-ṡaḋ 's ḃí aḃráin a's dánta binne
  Air tír 's air tonn d'a sgeiṫ gan sgíṫ,
'S aig líonaḋ aigne na sluaġ le luinne,
  D'a m-bárr ni fuair tu aċt briseaḋ croiḋe.

III.

Cia ḃeiḋeaḋ a feiṫeaḋ, 'ċruit ċrom, air luaṫ-sruṫ,
  'O do ṫrom-teudaiḃ, de ċeoltaiḃ binn':
'O ṡuiseog maidne, ḃeiḋeaḋ ċo trátaṁail saor-guṫ,
  'N áit géire aig éagcaoin a h-aoise air linn.
Ciannos agaid'd air son saoirs' do ġaeṫe.
  Mo ċruit féin dilis, air a b-fuil agam gráḋ,
'S an ċraoḃ, le n-gléasaim do ċum a's d' ḟéiṫe,
  Gur fleásg tá sigte sí le slaḃraiḋe a's bláṫ.

MY GENTLE HARP.

Air—*The Caoine or Dirge.*

I.

My gentle Harp! once more I waken
  The sweetness of thy slumbering strain;
In tears our last farewell was taken,
  And now in tears we meet again.
No light of song hath o'er thee broken,
  But like those harps whose heavenly skill
Of slavery, dark as thine, have spoken—
  Thou hang'st upon the willow still.

II.

And yet, since last thy chord resounded,
  An hour of peace and triumph came,
And many an ardent bosom bounded
  With hopes—that now are turn'd to shame.
Yet even then while peace was singing
  Her halcyon song o'er land and sea,
Though joy and hope to others bringing,
  She only brought new tears to thee.

III.

Then, who can ask for notes of pleasure,
  My drooping harp, from chords like thine?
Alas, the lark's gay morning measure
  As ill would suit the swan's decline!
Or how shall I, who love, who bless thee,
  Invoke thy breath for freedom's strains,
When ev'n the wreaths in which I dress thee
  Are sadly mix'd—half flow'rs, half chains?

IV.

Aċt ċugam, 's má tá ann do ċum, tá aig feóċan,
  Aon ġuṫ aṁain siansa naċ b-fuil faoi suan,
Cosmuiġ dam-sa sé, a's tabair fios d'a ḃeoḋaċan,
  Gur binn do ċeolta lár bróin, 's gur buan—
Gur aoibhinn seinnear tú a lár na g-crónaċ,
  Tria bíḋeas fonn luinneaċ d'a ġabail go grinn,
Mar ioṁáiġ Meaṁnoin bríste, béiḋir go brónaċ
  Trí reisos 's trí ḟasaċ go h-aonaras, binn.

AIG SNÁṀ D'AR LOING ANN AĠAIḊ GAOṪ TEANN'.

Fonn—An cailín d' fág me 'mo ḋiaiġ.

I.

Aig snáṁ d'ar loing ann aġaiḋ gaoṫ' teann',
  Le' raiḃ a seolta líonta,
Do ċíḋfeaḋ an briat a steaċ ó'n g-crann
  Cum an ċuain, 'd' fág sí, sínte.
Mar sud is mall ar siúbal 's an t-sliġe
  'O áras ġráḋaċ ar g-cáirde,
Air a n-iompuiġeann claonta úṁal' ar g-croiḋe,
  Mar an long-brat sgaoilte ann áirde.

II.

Aig meaḃrúġaḋ an am', ċuaiḋ ṫart mar ceo
  Neaṁ-ḃríġṁar, 'bunn na fléiḋe;
Bíḋeann brón a's gáirdeoċas síor-ḃeo,
  'G a measgaḋ lár ar g-cleiḃe;
'S 'nuair dúisiġeann ceolta flaṫ 's an b-fléiḋ,
  Gaċ cáilíḋeaċt óg a's ċroiḋaṁail—
D'ar fan 'nnar n-diaiġ, bíḋeann cuaċ air leiṫ
  'Dul ṫart, 's 'g a ól go saoiṫaṁail.

IV.

But come, if yet thy frame can borrow
One breath of joy—oh! breathe for me,
And show the world in chains and sorrow,
How sweet thy music still can be;
How gaily, ev'n 'mid gloom surrounding,
Thou yet canst wake at pleasure's thrill—
Like Memnon's broken image sounding,
'Mid desolation tuneful still!

AS SLOW OUR SHIP.

Air—*The girl I left behind me.*

I.

As slow our ship her foamy track
Against the wind was cleaving,
Her trembling pennant still look'd back
To the dear isle 't was leaving.
So loath we part from all we love,
From all the links that bind us;
So turn our hearts where'er we rove,
To those we've left behind us.

II.

When, round the bowl, of vanish'd years
We talk, with joyous seeming,—
With smiles, that might as well be tears,
So faint, so sad their beaming;
While mem'ry brings us back again
Each early tie that twin'd us,
Oh! sweet 's the cup that circles then
To those we 've left behind us.

III.

A d-tírṫiḃ coigríġeaċa, an trá,
Do ċíḋmuid innse 's gleannta;
'S gaċ níḋ faoi ḃláṫ, aċt carḃa gráḋ
'S an coimgioll caoṁ do fantuiġ;
Buḋ mór an sólás air ar g-croiḋe,
'Gur bárr air aoiḃneas saoġalta,
Dá m-beiḋeaḋ súd againn le n-ar m-biṫ
Ann aon-ḟeaċt cáirde 's gaolta.

IV.

Mar siúḃlaċ soir, aig aṁarc siar,
Go mall aig teaċt na h-oiḋċe,
Aig breaċnuġaḋ air an lá air siar
Roiṁ ċuluġaḋ uaiḋe ċoiḋċe:
Mar súd, d' eis teilgean siar ar n-dearc,
O ḃruaċaiḃ garr' na h-uaiṁe,
Tig lóċran geal na h-óige searc'
Tre neulta aoise a's cúṁa.

'NUAIR 'SA G-CRÉ BEIḊEAS AN CARAD.

Fonn—Treunaḋ Liomnaiġ.

I.

'Nuair 'sa g-cré beiḋeas an carad, air raiḃ agat gráḋ,
Biḋeaḋ a lóċta 's a luaimneaċt fágta 's a g-cill;
Nó, ó 'n táiṁ trom, a ḃ-fuil ann, ma togṫar an sgáṫ,
Caoin iad gan gleo, 's an sgáṫ 'súr orra sil.
Aċt, ó má ta brónaċ le cuiṁnuġaḋ an sgeul,
Gur ċuluiġ le caṫuġaḋ ó'n t-solus a ċroiḋe,
Is aoiḃin an ċuiṁnuġaḋ go m-buḋ tu-sa an reul,
'Do ḟoilsiġ an a baile fe lár dúḃan, 'sa t-sliġe.

III.

And when in other climes we meet
  Some isle or vale enchanting,
Where all looks flow'ry, wild, and sweet,
  And nought but love is wanting;
We think how great had been our bliss,
  If heaven had but assigned us
To live and die in scenes like this,
  With some we 've left behind us.

IV.

As trav'llers oft look back at eve,
  When eastward darkly going,
To gaze upon that light they leave
  Still faint behind them glowing,—
So, when the close of pleasure's day
  To gloom hath near consign'd us,
We turn to catch one fading ray
  Of joy that 's left behind us.

WHEN COLD IN THE EARTH.

AIR—*Limerick's Lamentation.*

I.

When cold in the earth lies the friend thou hast lov'd,
  Be his faults and his follies forgot by thee then;
Or, if from their slumber the veil be remov'd,
  Weep o'er them in silence, and close it again.
And oh! if 't is pain to remember how far
  From the pathways of light he was tempted to roam,
Be it bliss to remember that thou wert the star
  That arose on his darkness, and guided him home.

II.

Uait-se 's ó d' áille, gan smal air, do lás,
An t-eagna do ċlaon sé ċum fíor-ġraḋ go mór,
Aig aireaṁ do spioraid lonraċ a ċas,
'O na ioġṁaiġṫe táir', d'a raiḃ taḃ'rṫa go leor.
Air snuṫa a ḃeaṫa duḃ, measgṫa le gaoṫ,
Ṫainic mar ċúnas geal, sáṁ air an tuinn,
'S ma ḃí claonaḋ a lacṫe le leus aoiḃaṁail buiḋe
'S uait 'síolruiġ an solus do sgeiṫ le n-a linn.

III.

'S ciú d' éiroċaḋ ó ḃaoise na h-oige duḃ-neul,
'S ciú seolóċaḋ air seaċrán 's áir seaċṁal sé, breug,
Aig, iompuġaḋ air an glóir, ḃí 's na roise úd mar reul,
Gan muil scaraḋ an ḃaoise 's an seaċrán go h-eug.
Mar sagairt na gréine, le sgalaḋ de 'n lá,
Briseas a lasaḋ na h-altóra ḃí sṁúdaṁail faoi ċeo:
Ma ḃí suḃailce, aon tamal, lag-ḃríġaċ, faoi sgáṫ,
D' iompuiġ air a smigeaḋ 's ḃí lasta go beo.

BI CINTE GIḊ FÁGṪA TÁIR.

Fonn—Caisleán Tir-eon.

I.

Bi cinte giḋ fágṫa táir, ċo fad 's ḃeiḋeas me beo,
Naċ n-euloċaiḋ do ċuṁan as mo ċroiḋe stiġ go deo;
Níos dilse faoi ṫrom-ḃrón, faoi ḋuḃaċan 's faoi ṡian,
'Na tirċe is téagraiġe air soilsiġeann an ġrian.

II.

Da m-beiḋeaḋ mar b' ait liom, mór, árd, saor, a ġraḋ,
De 'n ṁuir, sgaiṫ na seoide; de 'n tír, sgaiṫ na m-blaṫ.
Do ċumáċta buḋ réiṁeaċ liom féin ḃeiṫ 'g a luaḋ,
Aċt mo ċionn ort ní ṁeudóċaḋ do ċéim, no do ṫuaḋ.

II.

From thee and thy innocent beauty first came
  The revealings, that first taught true love to adore,
To feel the bright presence, and turn him with shame
  From the idols he blindly had knelt to before.
O'er the waves of a life, long benighted and wild,
  Thou cam'st like a soft golden calm o'er the sea;
And if happiness purely and glowingly smiled,
  On his evening horizon, the light was from thee.

III.

And tho', sometimes, the shade of past folly would rise,
  And tho' falsehood again should allure him to stray,
He but turn'd to the glory that dwelt in those eyes,
  And the folly, the falsehood soon vanished away.
As the priests of the Sun, when their altar grew dim,
  At the day-beam alone could its lustre repair;
So, if virtue a moment grew languid in him,
  He but flew to that smile, and rekindled it there.

REMEMBER THEE! YES.

Air—*Castle Tirowen.*

I.

Remember thee! yes, while there 's life in this heart,
It shall never forget thee, all lorn as thou art;
More dear in thy sorrow, thy gloom, and thy showers,
Than the rest of the world in their sunniest hours.

II.

Wert thou all that I wish thee—great, glorious, and free,
First flow'r of the earth, and first gem of the sea,
I might hail thee with prouder, with happier brow,
But, oh! could I love thee more deeply than now?

III.

Aig teaċt, le gcur-ċuibre, do d' ḟuil go tiúġ, teann,
'S se foilsiġeann a g-cúram níos teagaraġ do ċlann,
Mar an t-ál anns an b-fásac 's a nead teasgraċ teo,
'G a g-congḃáil le fuil bronn a máṫar fíor-ḃeo.

Fiġ ṫart air taoḃ.

Fonn—Nora an ċiste.

I.

Fiġ ṫart air taoḃ
Na cuaiċe, craoḃ
Is glaise de ġrean faoiṫeamail:
Go neaṁ na reul,
Noċt súd le gaol,
Tréigsint dream' neaṁċroiḋamal.
Ma ḃiḋeann an gráḋ,
'Stiġ filte a sgáṫ,
An t-suarcais 'n aġaiḋ a tréiġte,
Le dóiġ bí teann,
Co'ad 's ḃeiḋeas fíon ann,
Le m-báiṫfamuid a ġaeṫe.

III.

No; thy chains as they rankle, thy blood as it runs,
But make thee more painfully dear to thy sons,
Whose hearts, like the young of the desert-bird's nest,
Drink love in each life-drop that flows from thy breast.

WREATHE THE BOWL.

AIR—*Nora án Kiste.*

I.

Wreathe the bowl
With flow'rs of soul,
The brightest Wit can find us;
We 'll take a flight
Tow'rds Heav'n to-night,
And leave dull earth behind us.
Should Love amid
The wreaths be hid,
Which Mirth, th' enchanter, brings us.
No danger fear,
While wine is near,
We 'll drown him if he stings us,
Then wreathe the bowl
With flow'rs of soul,
The brightest Wit can find us;
We 'll take a flight
Tow'rds Heav'n to-night,
And leave dull earth behind us.

II.

Buḋ gnáṫaċ aig flaiṫ,
Na ndia, le sgaiṫ
Deoċ neaṁḋa 'ḃeiṫ 'g a m-beoḋaċan,
'S tá air ar sliġe,
An sgaiṫ ud diġe,
Do ṁeasgaḋ féin ar n-dóċain:—
Mar so, tóig fíon,
An cuaċ suas líon,
'S liḋeaḋ timċioll suile sgiaṁaṁail',
'S le gaeṫe grinn,
Las suas an linn,
'S feuċ deoċ na n-Dia go céim'ail.

III.

Taḃ'r fios cia an faṫ,
A n-deárnaiḋ triaṫ,
An cuaċ le gaineaṁ líonaḋ,
'Nuair is luaiṫe sruṫ,
An ḟíon', 'sa ċruṫ,
Is deirc é, niḋ naċ iongaḋ:
'O! duinn é brionn,
Le sinig 's le fonn,
'S de'n sgála déanfam' roimte,
'Gur beiḋiḋ go fras,
Dá ṫuile teaċt as
'S an dá ṫaoḃ lán go cinte.

II.

'T was nectar fed.
Of old, 't is said,
Their Junos, Joves, Apollos ;
But Man may brew
His nectar too,
The rich receipt 's as follows :
Take wine like this,
Let looks of bliss
Around it well be blended,
Then bring Wit's beam
To warm the stream,
And there 's your nectar, splendid!
So wreathe the bowl, etc.

III.

Say, why did Time
His glass sublime
Fill up with sands unsightly,
When wine, he knew,
Runs brisker through,
And sparkles far more brightly?
Oh! lend it us,
And, smiling thus,
The glass in two we 'll sever,
Make pleasure glide
In double tide,
And fill both ends for ever.
Then wreathe the bowl, etc.

NA DEARMAD AN ḞAIṪ.

Fonn—Cúṁa Aċruim.

I.

Na dearmad an ḟaiṫ air ar síneaḋ
  Sgaiṫ déiġionaċ na laoċ anns an ár,
Uile imṫiġṫe: 'gur sinn-ne 'g a g-caoineaḋ
  'S an ċéim tá 'sa g-cré leo fá lár.

II.

O! da m-b' féidir ó'n g-cré, glaoḋaċ ċum gliaṫa
  Air na gaisgiḋiġ, tá cugṫa a suan,
Aig iniṫ lé lann a's le sgiaṫa
  Air son saoirse arís go síor-ḃuan.

III.

Dá b-fáġfamuis na cuiḃreaċa 'ḃriseaḋ,
  D' fáisg dian-ċeannas orainn, 's ní fann,
O! is cinte air ṫíorán go g-clisfeaḋ
  'N-aġaiḋ céirt, a g-cur orainn go teann.

IV.

Aċt tá ċeart—a's giḋ molta 'sna sgeultaiḃ,
  'S na stairṫiḃ, tá ḃreugaċ no fíor,
Béiḋ an buaḋ-oirc faoi ṁallaċt 's faoi neultaiḃ,
  Gníḋear saltairt air ċroiḋṫiḃ bí saor.

V.

Is annsa an uaiṁ nó lann-slaḃraiḋe,
  B-fuil lóċrann ċlú laoċrá tír-ġraḋaċ,
'Na buaiḋ ċraoḃ an méid á ḃeiḋear meaḃruiġ'
  Fá ċuiṁne air ċreaċ saoirse, go ḃráṫ.

FORGET NOT THE FIELD.

Air—The Lamentation of Limerick.

I.

Forget not the field where they perish'd,
  The truest, the last of the brave,
All gone—and the bright hope we cherished,
  Gone with them, and quench'd in their grave!

II.

Oh! could we from death but recover
  Those hearts, as they bounded before,
In the face of high heaven to fight over
  That combat for Freedom once more.

III.

Could the chain for an instant be riven,
  Which tyranny flung round us then,
Oh! 't is not in Man nor in Heaven
  To let tyranny bind us again.

IV.

But 't is past; and tho' blazon'd in story
  The name of our victor may be,
Accurst is the march of that glory
  Which treads o'er the hearts of the free.

V.

Far dearer the grave or the prison,
  Illum'd by one patriot name,
Than the trophies of all who have risen
  On Liberty's ruins to fame.

O! do lannaiḃ an am', tá a g-cian.

Fonn—Ní 'l fios air.

I.

O! do lannaiḃ an am', tá a g-cian,
O! do na gairgiḋiḃ cliúċaċ',
Do ċosain ceart, mar sgaiṫ na ḃ-fian,
'S do ḃí lé dian-oiric, cúiteaċ!
Na feara fíor' go fóill nár ṁill
Tair-seoide caisleán ríġeaṁail,
Aċt sealḃ céim, do saoṫruiġ a's ṫuill
Le crúḋaċt a's cáiliḋeaċt saiṫeaṁail.
O! do lannaiḃ an am', tá a g-cian,
O! do na gairgiḋiḃ cliuċaċ',
Do ċosain ceart, mar sgaiṫ na ḃ-fian,
'S do ḃí lé dian-oiric, cúiteaċ!

II.

O! do na ríġṫiḃ, 'ḃí 'nuair sin ann,
O! d'a mór-ċúis réimeaṁail;
D'a g-cúṁdaċ ní raiḃ dún no lann,
Aċt láṁa laoċra céimeaṁail!
'Nuair ḃí sgiaṫ uċta dluṫ, mar ġeall
Air coinġioll teáġarac croiḋṫe,
Aig cosaint ó gaċ masla 's feall
Ard-ċaṫair gráḋaċ na ríġṫe!
O! do na ríġṫiḃ, 'ḃí 'nuair sin ann,
O! d'a mór-ċúis réimeaṁail;
D'a g-cúṁdaċ ní raiḃ dún no lann,
Aċt láṁa laoċra céimeaṁal'!

OH! FOR THE SWORDS.

AIR—*Name unknown.*

I.

Oh! for the Swords of former time!
Oh! for the men who bore them!
When, arm'd for Right, they stood sublime,
And tyrants crouch'd before them!
When pure yet, ere courts began
With honours to enslave him,
The best honours worn by man
Were those which virtue gave him.
Oh! for the swords, etc.

II.

Oh! for the Kings who flourished then!
Oh! for the pomp that crown'd them,
When hearts and hands of free-born men
Were all the ramparts round them!
When, safe built on bosoms true,
The throne was but the centre
Round which Love a circle drew,
That Treason durst not enter.
Oh! for the kings, etc.

SIÚḂAL, SIÚḂAL A LOING.

Fonn—Dran-dán na Bainne.

I.

Siúḃal, siúḃal a loing, gan sgáṫ 'sa t-sruṫ,
Réir mar seolfas ṫú, an ġaoṫ,
Ní ḃéiḋmuid báiṫte a m-brón ċo duḃ,
A's ḃímar ċeana, feasda ċoiḋċe—
'S se an glór do ḃrisear ó gaċ tonn;
Giḋ an bás ḃeiṫ faoi n-ar smígeaḋ 'nna luiḋe,
Ní'l sinn fuar, cealgaċ mar an drong,
Ar slad a sing' do ċuid ' do ċroiḋe.

II.

Siúḃal leat, siúḃal leat, gan sgiṫ, gan suan,
Triḋ síon, 's triḋ ciúnas, lár na sráiġ',
An ṁuir is buairṫe, is ionnan 's cuan
Do 'n te d' fág droċ-ċroiḋṫe air tráiġ
No—buailtear sinn air talaṁ bán,
Air nár ṫuit gaċ fir an ċam-ċroiḋe,
Aig buaireaḋ saoġail de suaircas lán—
Déan ann, 's ná déan go d-ti sin, sgiṫ.

MA ḂEIR SAṀAILT BRÓNA.

Fonn—Air an m-baile so tá an Cúilin.
—No—
B 'fearr liom 'na Eirinn.

I.

Ma ḃeir saṁailt bróna 'gur fior-cruṫe cléiḃe
Aon comarṫa cinte air ḋáiṁ agus gaol
Is dearḃṫa gur uait-se, a ṫruaġ-ḋeoraiḋ sléiḃe
Naoṁ Sion, do ṫainic sliocṫ Eireann a's síol.

SAIL ON, SAIL ON.

AIR—*The Humming of the Ban.*

I.

Sail on, sail on, thou fearless bark:
Wherever blows the welcome wind,
It cannot lead to scenes more dark,
More sad than those we leave behind.
Each wave that passes seems to say:
"Though death beneath our smile may be,
Less cold we are, less false than they,
Whose smiling wreck'd thy hopes and thee".

II.

Sail on, sail on: through endless years—
Through calm—through tempest—stop no more.
The stormiest sea 's a resting place
To him who leaves such hearts on shore.
Or—if some desert land we meet,
Where never yet false-hearted men
Profan'd a world that else were sweet,
Then rest thee, bark, but not till then.

YES, SAD ONE OF SION.

AIR—*In this Village is the Cuilin; or, I'd Rather than Ireland.*

I.

Yes, sad one of Sion! if closely resembling,
In shame and in sorrow, thy wither'd-up heart—
If drinking, deep, deep, of the same "cup of trembling",
Could make us thy children, our parent thou art.

II.

Mar ṫu tá ar ríġeaċt faoi ġeur-ċeannas briste
'Gur tuitte ó n-a ceann ta an ċróin-ḟleasg 'nna luiḋe,
Tá a bailte 's a sráide mar ḟasaċ bán sgriosta
S a g-ceart lár an lae féin, tá a grian 'neis dul faoi.

III.

Mar do ċlan, tá a deoraiḋe lár dóċais ag filleaḋ,
Fáġail báis fad o'n m-baile a ḃeiṫ ann, buḋ se 'mian,
Mar do ṡlioċt, tá a slioċt-san lárduḃ-ḃróin na cille,
A meaṁraḋ laeṫe lonraċ' tá baiṫte a g-cian.

IV.

'S dual a bairteaḋ "bean ságṫe", mar ṫusa 'n am ársa,
Tá a h-uaisle 'na sgláḃaiḋe 'gur a treun-ḟir gan buaiḋ,
"S na ceolta is binne do ṫig ó n-a cláirsaiġ,
Sé is samail dóiḃ osnaiġeal na gaoiṫe air uaiṁ.

V.

Aċt fuair tú do ċúntuġaḋ 's ḃi an máraċ a soilsuġaḋ
Do ṫig 'néis an duḃaċam d'a ḟad' i an oiḋċe,
'S an ríġ-ḟlaṫ do ġread ṫu,—fuaḋ an naṁaid a soilsuġaḋ
Mar ġioléaċ ta briste os do ċoṁair gan aon ḃriġ.

VI.

Oir an ċuaċ searḃ ḃeirfeaḋ an óir-ċaṫair línte,
Ḃi 'ga cur le n-a beul féin 's buḋ cóir, ceart, an ċríoċ,
'S ċur gairdeas air na daoine, faoi n-a geur ċeannas sínte,
An uaill ó n-a ċallaiḋ 's ó n-a luingis an sgrúoċ.

VII.

Uair do ṫuit malaċt neiṁe, ḃi a d-táirge, go ballaċ
Air a ceanaiḋe 's air a ceanfairt luċt-ċreaċta go trom,
'S faoi léir-sgrios fa ḋeire 's aig cnuṁóg faoi ḟalaċ,
Ḃi ban-ríġean na ríġaċt' 'g a saltairt go lom.

II.

Like thee doth our nation lie conquered and broken,
And fall'n from her head is the once royal crown;
In her streets, in her halls, desolation hath spoken,
And "while it is day yet, her sun hath gone down".

III.

Like thee doth her exile, 'mid dreams of returning,
Die far from the home it were life to behold;
Like thine do her sons, in the day of their mourning,
Remember the bright things that bless'd them of old.

IV.

Ah! well may we call her, like thee, "the forsaken",
Her boldest are vanquish'd, her proudest are slaves;
And the harps of her minstrels, when gayest they waken,
Have breathings as sad as the wind over graves.

V.

Yet hadst thou thy vengeance—yet came there the morrow,
That shines out, at last, on the longest dark night,
When the sceptre that smote thee with slav'ry and sorrow,
Was shiver'd at once, like a reed, in thy sight.

VI.

When that cup, which, for others, the proud Golden City
Had brimm'd full of bitterness, drench'd her own lips,
And the world she had trampled on, heard, without pity,
The howl in her halls, and the cry from her ships.

VII.

When the curse heaven keeps for the haughty came over
Her merchants rapacious, her rulers unjust,
And—a ruin, at last, for the earth-worm to cover,—
The Lady of Kingdoms lay low in the dust.

ÓL AS AN G-CUAĊ SO.

Fonn—Patruic O'Rafairte.

I.

Ól as an g-cuaċ so, óir béarfaiḋ tu sraid
   Níos ar gaċ deor dé, 'nn aġaiḋ aicid a's euslan;
Na traċt air an gean-deoċ, ḃi aig Elin, mar ċaraid,
   Ní raiḃ an cuaċ sin aċt ran-sgeul; so 'n sgala ḃ-fuil cial ann.
Ḃlas ar an m-bollóg air a ḃár a tá lonraċ
   Ma 's mian leat an saoġal so do ḋíbirt, 's a neulta
Aċt trom-ḟaisc gaċ braon dé, le croiḋe naċ m-beiḋ sganraċ
   Ma 's áil leat ḃeiṫ togṫa ċo h-árd leis na reulta.
Cur ṫart an cuaċ; óir ḃeurfaiḋ tu sraid
   Níos ar gaċ deor dé 'nn aġaid aiciḋ a's euslan
Na traċt air an gean deoċ, ḃi aig Elin, mar ċaraid,
   Ni raiḃ an cuaċ sin aċt ran-sgeul, so an sgala ḃ-fuil cial ann.

II.

Go fóil riaṁ aon gean deoċ ċo briġṁar níor measgaḋ,
   Le n-ar ceudfaiḋ a ċluanuġaḋ, mar an sgála so líonṁar,
Do tionsgnaḋ a ḋraoċta, an tráṫ ḃi faoi ḃ-fascaḋ
   An grán borrṫa, sgiaṁaċ, faoi teas foġṁair grianṁair:
An rud 'n éis le téagar an t-saṁraiḋ, ḃeiṫ buiḋe, bán,
   'Sgeiṫeaḋ balaḋ 'gur blaṫ an t-séasuir buḋ tearṁaiġe,
Ḃi silt ar an suġ ud, 'tá mór iongantaċ, fór- lan
   Cum croiḋṫe do ḃeoċan, ḃeiḋeaḋ fuaruiġṫe d'a carḃa,
O an g-cuaċ mar sid ól óir ḃeurfaiḋ tu sraid
   Níos ar ga'ċ deor dé 'nn aġaiḋ aicid a's euslan,
Na traċt air an gean-deoċ ḃi aig Eilin mar ċaraid
   Ni raiḃ an cuaċ sin aċt ran-sgeul, so an sgala ḃ-fuil cial ann.

III.

Ci b' ḟeidir—aċt air so ni dualtraċt a coiḋċe—
   Mar an coire 'm-briḋeann gear caille, faireaḋ air, go caoiḋaṁail
Gur raiḃ an gean-deoċ so 'g a ṫarraing san oiḋċe
   Aċt ni laige a ḃriġ sa ḟe ṫeaċt go neaṁ-ḋliġaṁail.

DRINK OF THIS CUP

AIR—*Paddy O'Rafferty.*

I.

Drink of this cup: you 'll find there 's a spell in
Its every drop 'gainst the ills of mortality—
Talk of the cordial that sparkled for Helen,
Her cup was a fiction, but this is reality.
Would you forget the dark world we are in,
Only taste of the bubble that gleams on the top of it;
But would you rise above earth, till akin
To immortals themselves, you must drain every drop of it.
Send round the cup; for, oh! there 's a spell in
Its every drop 'gainst the ills of mortality.
Talk of the cordial that sparkled for Helen,
Her cup was a fiction, but this is reality.

II.

Never was philter form'd with such power
To charm and bewilder as this we are quaffing;
Its magic began when, in Autumn's rich hour,
As a harvest of gold in the fields it stood laughing.
There having, by nature's enchantment, been fill'd
With the balm and the bloom of her kindliest weather,
This wonderful juice from its core was distill'd,
To enliven such hearts as are here brought together!
Then drink of the cup: you 'll find there 's a spell in
Its every drop 'gainst the ills of mortality.
Talk of the cordial that sparkled for Helen,
Her cup was a fiction, but this is reality.

III.

And though, perhaps—but breathe it to no one—
Like the caldron the witch brews at midnight so awful,
In secret this philter was first taught to flow on,
Yet 't is n't less potent for being unlawful.

Naċ cuma, ciḋ fanann air fós, fuiġilleaċ balaḋ
  An deataiġ o'n lasair 'ċug a ḃriġ 'maċ go ballaċ
Cuir an drúċda neaṁ-ċeadaṁail 'sa sgála tá falaṁ
  Béarfaid fuarcas as croiḋṫe tá annta faoi falaċ.
As an g-cuaċ mar sin ól, óir béarfaiḋ tu oraid
  Níos as gaċ deor dé, 'nn aġaiḋ aicid a's cuslán
Na traċt air an gean-deoċ ḃi aig Eilin, mar ċaraid,
  Ni raiḃ an cuaċ sin aċt ran-sgeul, so an sgala 'ḃ-fuil cial ann.

O! na taṫuiġ ċum fleiṫe.

Fonn—Planesti Iarḃain.

I.

O na ḃi tuṫuġaḋ ċum fleiṫe na lann'
  'N a g-cruinniġeann an t-óg 'gus luċt na baois'
Aċt tar liom féin 's gaḃfair crion-ḃláṫ ann,
  D' ḟoirsear níos feárr do do ḃrón 's do d' aois.
'Gus ġoḃfam' ar n-doċan deora teo
  'Gus ólfam' 'nn ar d-tost, as cuaċ faoi ċoṁar
Ar n-aoiḋe'—táis' ama ċuaiḋ ṫart go deo,
  'Gus ar sláinte go ṡuiliḃ a tá faoi 'n úir.

II.

Trá 'n cannaċ a ḃeiṫ go tiuġ a sgeiṫeaḋ
  'N ar d-timċioll, duilleoga críon' ó'n geug;
Do ġealtaiḃ fan', beiḋ cuaċ fa leiṫ,
  Do ċáirde cailte, d' aṫruiġ 'gus d' eug:
No, do 'n laḃral aig sgaraḋ a ċraoḃ
  Os cionn na h-áite duiḃe, mar sgáṫ;
Do na h-uaiṁiḃ olfam' tá le n-a ṫaoḃ
  Ḃ-fuil gaisciġ 'nn a luiḋe gan clu, gan bláṫ.

What though it may taste of the smoke of that flame,
  Which in silence extracted its virtues forbidden,
Fill up! there 's a fire in some hearts I could name,
  Which may work too its charm, though now lawless and hidden.
So drink of the cup! for, oh! there 's a spell in
  Its every drop 'gainst the ills of mortality.
Talk of the cordial that sparkled for Helen,
  Her cup was a fiction, but this is reality.

OH! BANQUET NOT.

AIR—*Planxty Irwine.*

I.

Oh! banquet not in those shining bowers,
  Where youth resorts; but come to me,
For mine 's a garden of faded flowers,
  More fit for sorrow, for age, and thee.
And there we shall have our feast of tears,
  And many a cup in silence pour—
Our guests, the shades of former years,
  Our toasts, to lips that bloom no more.

II.

Then, while the myrtle's withering boughs
  Their lifeless leaves around us shed,
We 'll brim the bowl to broken vows,
  To friends long lost, the chang'd, the dead.
Or, as some blighted laurel waves
  Its branches o'er the dreary spot,
We 'll drink to those neglected graves
  Where valour sleeps, unnamed, forgot.

'M-beiḋ an ċlarsaċ gan ceol.

Fonn—Caoine Ṁic Farlain.

I

'M-béiḋ an ċlarsaċ gan ceol, 'gus an ċeud ḟear ṫug clú,
D' ar d-tír 'nois uainn tógṫa, ó 'n t-saoġal so go deo,
M-béiḋ filiḋ na h-Eireann, air an uaiṁ gan aon luṫ,
B-fuil ann fear toisiġ 's déiġ'niġ d' a caraid neaṁ beo.

II.

Ní ḃeiḋ, 's caḋ gur fann fuaim anċeoil ó n-a ḃeul
Ciḋ a ċruit a ḃeiṫ baiṫte faoi ċeo, mar a ċroiḋe,
Béarfaiḋ fuagraḋ 'n ḋiaiġ sin, lár duḃaċan na neul
Tá air Eirinn, gur lonraċ an réult a ċuaiḋ faoi.

III.

Gaċ ceadfaḋ 'gus cáiliḋeaċt le 'g-cuirtear bárr
Maise air ḋaoine, anns an aigne úd ḃí cruinn,
Raiḃ 'áras 'nn ar measg féin, 'nna ċoṁnuiḋ ann ar lár,
'Gus cadruġaḋ 'nna ḋiaiġ sin, síol Aḋaiṁ gan roinn.

IV.

Cia se ġráḋuiġear Éire, no ḋearcas an re,
Ṫríd a staire lom', bána, aig eiruġe gan ceo.
Mar ċloġṫeaċ 'sa b-fasaċ, an áit a b-fuil se
'S an glóir tá 'nna ṫimċioll, le seisint go deo.

V.

Aon ḃall aṁain dealuiġṫe le lannair mór-ċáil,
O duḃaċán 's ó buile na g-cian ḃí gan céim.
'Nuair a d'Eiriġ 's a spreag le n-a ġaeṫe, Inis-fáil
'S tug ṫar teorann na sglaḃaċt', ċum saoirse árd-léim.

SHALL THE HARP THEN BE SILENT?

AIR—*MacFarlan's Lament.*

I.

Shall the Harp then be silent when he who first gave
  To our country a name, is withdrawn from all eyes?
Shall a minstrel of Erin stand mute by the grave
  Where the first—where the last of the Patriots lies?

II.

No! faint tho' the death-song may fall from his lips,
  Tho' his harp, like his soul, may with shadows be crost,
Yet, yet shall it sound, 'mid a nation's eclipse,
  And proclaim to the world what a star hath been lost.

III.

What a union of all affections and powers,
  By which life is exalted, embellish'd, refin'd,
Was embrac'd in that spirit, whose centre was ours,
  While its mighty circumference circled mankind.

IV.

Oh! who that loves Erin, or who that can see,
  Through the waste of her annals, that epoch sublime,
Like a pyramid rais'd in the desert, where he
  And his glory stand out to the eyes of all time.

V.

That one lucid interval, snatch'd from the gloom
  And the madness of ages, when, filled with his soul,
A nation o'erleap'd the dark bounds of her doom,
  And, for one sacred instant, touch'd Liberty's goal!

VI.

Cia an neaċ a d' éirtiġ a riaṁ le n-aġuṫ
'Gur fós ċoisc le lán-tuile 'bṙeiṫre a ṫart,
Raiḃ fíor-ṫobar Eireann a ruṫ ṫríd 'n na sruṫ
'S a folsuġaḋ 'ṁor-fairsnaċt 'gur fós a ṁor-neart.

VII.

Buan-ċaint teaċt le fána gan faillíḋ mar áṫan
A taosgaḋ air a ṫuille ciall doiṁin an ċroiḋe,
'S a tarraint ṫre seaṫan a ṫonna mór-lán
Dealraḋ 'gur cruaiḋ-ḃriġ na seoide ḃi faoi.

VIII.

Cia ċeadreaḋ se dealuiġṫe ó ċruinniġṫe, riaṁ,
Air a ṫeallaċ air ḃ' ansa leis gnáċ-coṁnuiġe ann,
'Measg crana 'ḃron Eire 's air lubaḋ gaċ craoḃ,
Aṁail claonṁar le geug-sleasg do ċur air a ċeann.

IX.

Teallaċ do ḃeir ċum ar g-cuiṁne, an fear
Do ṫeilg dé a ġaeṫe 's air a leanḃ do ḃlaoiġ,
Druidim leis gan seanraḋ, no eagla, ċo gar,
A falaċ a ḃeir féin leis, no treiṫe ḃeir gnaoi.

X.

Cia an neaċ do ḃí dearcaḋ air ḃuan-ċuairt an reul
Ṫríd ṁolaḋ, no oilḃeim, naċ ḃ-facaiḋ go fíor,
Biḋeaḋ soilseaċ le glóire, no fáluiġṫe faoi neul,
Se árduiġṫe os cionn a ċo-ama go fíor.

XI.

Cia an cruinniġaḋ de ḃeusa ḃeir maise d' ar m-biḋ?
Ard-ċeim ḃiḋeas ion-ṁolta, 'gus cuman ḃiḋeas sáiṁ,
'S a ṡamuil le cuṁaċt a's neaṁ-gangad a ċroiḋe,
An leanḃ 's an ċaor-splanca toirne 'nn a láiṁ,

VI.

Who, that ever hath heard him, hath drunk at the source
  Of that wonderful eloquence, all Erin's own,
In whose high-thoughted daring, the fire, and the force,
  And the yet untam'd spring of his spirit, are shown.

VII.

An eloquence rich, wheresoever its wave
  Wander'd free and triumphant with thoughts that shone through,
As clear as the brook's "stone of lustre", and gave,
  With flash of the gem, its solidity too.

VIII.

Who that ever approach'd him, when free from the crowd,
  In a home full of love, he delighted to tread,
'Mong the trees which a nation had giv'n, and which bow'd
  As if each brought a new civic crown for his head.

IX.

That home, where, like him who, as fable hath told,
  Put rays from his brow, that his child might come near,
Every glory forgot, the most wise of the old
  Became all that the simplest and youngest hold dear.

X.

Is there one who hath thus, through his orbit of life,
  At a distance observed him, through glory, through blame,
In the calm of retreat, in the grandeur of strife,
  Whether shining or clouded, still high and the same.

XI.

Such a union of all that enriches life's hour—
  Of the sweetness we love, of the greatness we praise—
As that type of simplicity blended with power,
  A child with a thunder-bolt only pourtrays.

XII

Ní'l aon ċroiḋe do ċeadruiġ se naċ ḃ-fuil, faoi ċuma,
Fa gur ealuiġ ann aonaċt le n-a ġlóir uainn, an faoi,
'S naċ ngulfiḋ air a ṫuama tá tógṫa ó'n uaim,
Ḃ-fuil sgaiṫ na ḃ-fear eagna 'gur treanṁar', 'nna luiġe.

O! 'n t-aṁarc tóigfaḋ croiḋe.

Fonn—Planerti Sudloiḋ.

I.

O! 'n t-aṁarc ṫóigfaḋ croiḋe,
An reul moċ ṫriḋ an oiḋċe
Lasaḋ clogaiḋ 's lann
Na Sluaġta teann,
'Gur eitiḋ 'rinc 's na gaoṫa
Oir tá treun croiḋṫe léimnuġaḋ,
'S guṫ aḋairc an ċaṫ ' aig géimnuġaḋ,
Le fuaim an gleo
Do ḃearfaḋ cró,
Gan teiṫaḋ coiḋċe ó 'n dréimne
O! an t-aṁarc ṫóigfaḋ croiḋe,
An reul moċ ṫriḋ an oiḋċe
Lasaḋ clogaiḋ 's lann
Na Sluaġta teann.
'Gur eitiḋ 'rinc 's na gaoṫa

II.

Ní'l a g-clogaiḃ, no 'nn eitiḋ aon ḃriġ,
Fiafruiġ tu de 'o dian-riġ,
Ḃ-fuil. measg na réim',
Tá faoi n-a ċéim,
Toġa fir mar fuḋ air aon ċroiḋe,
Fág. aig luċt tá santuġaḋ mór-ċuis.

XII.

Oh! no; not a heart that e'er knew him but mourns
  Deep, deep o'er the grave, where such glory is shrin'd,
O'er a monument Fame will preserve 'mong the urns
  Of the wisest, the bravest, the best of mankind.

OH! THE SIGHT ENTRANCING.

AIR—*Planxty Sudley.*

I.

Oh! the sight entrancing,
When morning's beam is glancing
    O'er files array'd
    With helm and blade.
And plumes in the gay wind dancing!
When hearts are all high beating,
And the trumpet's voice repeating
    That song whose breath
    May lead to death,
But never to retreating!
Oh! the sight entrancing,
When morning's beam is glancing
    O'er files array'd
    With helm and blade,
And plumes in the gay wind dancing!

II.

Yes, 't is not helm nor feather—
For ask yon despot whether
    His plumèd bands
    Could bring such hands
And hearts as ours together.
Leave pomps to those who need 'em—

Bíḋeaḋ saoirse aig fear mar Leor-duais
'S ní'l triáil gan bríġ,
Tá snaiṁ 'n eir sriġ
Naċ n-ionnsoċaiḋ se le fór-ġnuis.
Téiḋeann geur-lann' na buaiḋ,
Ṫriḋ clogaiḋ 's ballaiḋ cruaid'.
Ċum saoirse ní'l bríġ,
Mar congial croiḋe
A mór-neart cliaḃ' nna luiḋe.
O! 'n t-aṁarc tóigfaḋ croiḋe
An peul moċ ṫriḋ an oiḋċe,
Lasaḋ clogaiḋ 's lann'
Na Sluaiġte teann,
'Gur eitiḋ surc 'san gaoṫ.

'Ċaoiṁ Innisfaillin.

Fonn—An t-óg fear Ceansa.

I

'Caoiṁ Innisfáillin! bi tu slán
Bíḋeaḋ ort grían-leus agus síṫ,
Do ḋeise luaḋ, do ṫig le lán,
Aċt ó, a ṁoṫuġaḋ, 's le mo ċroiḋe.

II.

Slán, ċaoiṁ Innisfállin, bí
'S bíḋeaḋ an leus do ṫimċioll buan,
Ċo saiṁ a's ċuit le teaċt na h-oiḋċe
Ar ḋearc me 'r d' ins'-siġe, 'gur cuan.

III.

Ḃí tu ro ḃreáġ aig neaċ 'san am
Ar dual dó airtir anns a' t-sliġe
Le sramairt siubal ṫri ḃealaiġ cam'
Do d' ḟágail aonrac, feasda, ċoiḋċe.

Adorn but Man with freedom,
And proud he braves
The gaudiest slaves
That crawl where monarchs lead 'em.
The sword may pierce the beaver,
Stone walls in time may sever:
'T is heart alone,
Worth steel and stone,
That keeps men free for ever!
Oh! the sight entrancing,
When morning's beam is glancing
O'er files array'd
With helm and blade,
And in Freedom's cause advancing

SWEET INNISFALLEN.

AIR—*The Captivating Youth.*

I.

Sweet Innisfallen, fare thee well,
May calm and sunshine long be thine!
How fair thou art let others tell,
While but to feel how fair is mine.

II.

Sweet Innisfallen, fare thee well,
And long may light around thee smile,
As soft as on that evening fell,
When first I saw thy fairy isle!

III.

Thou wert too lovely then for one,
Who had to turn to paths of care—
Who had through vulgar crowds to run,
And leave thee bright and silent there;

IV.

Gan ṫeaċt níos mó le ais do ṡruṫ,
  D'a ḃogaḋ air ṁuir an t-saoġail gan táṁ,
Dearcaḋ ċruḋ aislin ort 'sa' m-bruṫ.
  Mar ḃaile 'b-fuil a leaṫ faoi ṡlaṁ.

V.

'S feárr d' ḟágail mar tá me 'sa trá,
  A b-fuil ort sgarṫa eadaiġ duḃ'
Na neul, mar ṁaiġdean ann a blaṫ,
  A m-biḋeann faoi ḃrón a gne 's a cruṫ.

VI.

Oir ciḋ d' ionnan ni'l le fáġail
  A sgeiṁ, ní aṁail ṫú mar ḃí;
'S mar áit ṫu, falluiġṫe 'nois le sgáil,
  'N do ṫoróċaḋ neaċ, ḃeiḋeaḋ tursaċ, sgiṫ.

VII.

'Nna d' toróċaḋ sgiṫ ' geaḃfaḋ ann,
  Smuid mar ḃí 'b-parrṫas air an lá
Raiḃ cranna crom, mar tá gaċ crann
  Ar leat, faoi ḋeora 'gus faoi sgáṫ

VIII.

A gul, no smiġeaḋ Innis ḃreáġ!
  'S fos níos breaġa lán deora 's neul,
Tu ḃeiṫ faoi smíg ciḋ 's anaṁ an trá,
  Biḋeann si lonraċ, mar neaṁ-reul.

IX.

Mar ṡiad le 'r anaṁ sians' a m-biḋeann,
  A sasuġaḋ tra do ṫig. o g-croiḋe;
An gaċ is lonraiġe ċeilg an ġrian,
  Le taoḃ do lóċrain, tá gan brig.

IV.

No more along thy shores to come,
  But, on the world's dim ocean tost,
Dream of thee sometimes, as a home
  Of sunshine he had seen and lost!

V.

Far better in thy weeping hours,
  To part from thee, as I do now,
When mist is o'er thy blooming bow'rs,
  Like sorrow's veil on beauty's brow.

VI.

For, though unrivall'd still thy grace,
  Thou dost not look, as then, too blest,
But, in thy shadows, seem'st a place
  Where weary man might hope to rest—

VII.

Might hope to rest, and find in thee
  A gloom like Eden's, on the day
He left its shade, when every tree,
  Like thee, hung weeping o'er his way!

VIII.

Weeping or smiling, lovely isle!
  And still the lovelier for thy tears—
For tho' but rare thy sunny smile,
  'T is Heav'n's own glance, when it appears.

IX.

Like feeling hearts, whose joys are few,
  But, when indeed they come, divine,
The steadiest light the sun e'er threw
  Is lifeless to one gleam of thine.

Buḋ aon de na h-aislin'.

Fonn—abran na g-Coilte.

I.

Buḋ aon de na h-aislin' ḃeir ceol leis 'sa n-oiḋċe
Mar slaṁ eatrom saṁraiḋ dul trearsna ċar croiḋe
An ḟile ḃrúcas báiṫte le roiṁ-ṁeaṁair a g-ceo,
'S an saoġal aċt a ṁilseaċt uaiḋ ealuiġṫe go deo.

II.

Si an aill áine 'snaṁ cuige trearsna ó 'n toinn,
Le 'r gnaṫaċ do ḃeiṫ ċanaḋ creaċ' Eireann go binn;
'S ó innis glas Dinis go cuan glean' na g-craoḃ,
Ḃi gaeṫe an ġeur-aḋairc 'g a sgapaḋ air gaċ taoḃ.

III.

d'Eist co'ad 's ḃi an lag-fuaim a ċongḃuġaḋ le sgiṫ,
Os cionn na h-ard neide, 'raiḃ an t-iolar 'nn a luiḋe,
'S le eagla go n-eagfaḋ an sig-ċeol, do ġáir
Ḃinn-ċeol an mac-ala,—a tabairt air, fáir.

IV.

Do saoilfaḋ gaċ fan-ḟuaim nar ḃ' ḟeidir le cluas,
Do ċluinstáil go h-ísiol ḃeiṫ 'g a duraċt ṡuas,
Air barraiḃ na sliabta,—neaṁ áird na m-beann,
Raiḃ an ceol d' eug air talaṁ g' a aṫ-ḃeoḋaċan ann.

V.

Na tóig air, 's se aig éisteaċt le ceolta binn' buan',
Ṫug d' a ainm briġ áird le n-a ċosaint ó ṡuan
'S ó ḟostáċt an ḃáis;—da g-cluinfeaḋ stiġ beo,
'Mar sud air mac alla ḃéarfar d' ainm go deo.

'T WAS ONE OF THOSE DREAMS.

AIR—*The Song of the Woods.*

I.

'T was one of those dreams that by music are brought,
Like a bright summer haze, o'er the poet's warm thought—
When, lost in the future, his soul wanders on,
And all of this life, but its sweetness, is gone.

II.

The wild notes he heard o'er the water were those
He had taught to sing Erin's dark bondage and woes,
And the breath of the bugle now wafted them o'er
From Dinis' green isle to Glena's wooded shore.

III.

He listen'd—while high o'er the eagle's rude nest,
The lingering sounds on their way lov'd to rest;
And the echoes sung back from their full mountain quire,
As if loath to let song so enchanting expire.

IV.

It seem'd as if ev'ry sweet note, that died here,
Was again brought to life in some airier sphere,
Some heav'n in those hills, where the soul of the strain
That had ceas'd upon earth was awaking again.

V.

Oh! forgive, if, while list'ning to music, whose breath
Seem'd to circle his name with a charm against death,
He should feel a proud spirit within him proclaim,
"Even so shalt thou live in the echoes of Fame:

VI.

Mar súd da m-beiḋeaḋ báiṫte 'nois d' ainm faoi sgáil,
Brisfaḋ amaċ ann am tráṫamail, ó 'n smuid duḃ do ċáil,
'S tríḋ cianta fad ama, béid d' aḃrain 's do ṫuaḋ,
Le croiḋṫe 's guṫ Eireann 'g a g-canaḋ 's 'g a luaḋ.

AḂRAN INNISE FAIL.

Fonn—Pegiḋ ḃán.

I.

Do ṫainic ó ċríċ taoḃ ṫál de'n ḃ-fráiġ,
  'Gur tríd an ṁuir ṡiar go beo,
Sgaol a g-cuid seolta breáġ ó 'n tráiġ
  Ċum talṁán na Spáine teo.
'O' cá ḃ-fuil an Innis,—cnoċ ar sliġe
  Do facas dúinn a d-táiṁ
Do ṡeinn air maidin tra ḃí cóir-ġaoṫ
  'G a seolaḋ ṫríd an t-snáṁ

II.

Agus feuċ ḃ-fad uainn air ḃarr na d-tonn
  Ḃ-fuil lóċran soilseaċ glas,
Aṁail 's da m-beiḋeaḋ sínte faoi na m-bunn
  Smearóga soilseaċ' deas'
Si Innis Fáil; sí Innis Fáil!
  'Seinneaḋ ó 'n ṁuir go binn,
A g-coiṁnuiġeann an saor 's an treun réir cáil'
  Freagaḋ arís ó 'n toinn.

III.

'Nois d' iompuiġ ċum na soir-ṁuir searc
  Raiḃ rosg a n-Dé an lae
Teilgean go grianṁar air a ḋearc
  'Sgeiṫ air aer 's air uisg' a rae.

VI.

"Even so, tho' thy mem'ry should now die away,
"'T will be caught up again in some happier day,
"And the hearts and the voices of Erin prolong,
"Through the answering future, thy name and thy song".

SONG OF INNISFAIL.

AIR—*Peggy Bawn.*

I.

They came from a land beyond the sea,
  And now o'er the western main
Set sail, in their good ships, gallantly,
  From the sunny land of Spain.
"Oh! where 's the Isle we 've seen in dreams,
  "Our destin'd home or grave?"
Thus sung they, as by the morning beams,
  They swept th' Atlantic wave.

II.

And, lo, where afar o'er ocean shines
  A sparkle of radiant green,
As though in that deep lay emerald mines,
  Whose light thro' the wave was seen.
"'T is Innisfail! "'t is Innisfail!"
  Rings o'er the echoing sea;
While, bending to heav'n, the warriors hail
  That home of the brave and free.

III.

Then turn'd they unto the Eastern wave,
  Where now their Day-God's eye
A look of such sunny omen gave
  As lighted up sea and sky.

Aċt ni raiḃ aon deor air duil' no air ḟód
 No, air ṁuir, no air aer aon sgáil
Trá ṫóig ar sinsear 'nuas an sceód
 Air ċuan na h-Innse Fáil.

CIḊ GUR TAIR LIOM AN ḞLEIḊ.

Fonn—Slán leat Eamoin.

I

Ciḋ gur táir liom an ḟleiḋ, ḟuarais cuireaḋ a freastail,
 Gaḃfair tóġa' ḃ-fuil aig bord boċt le cur air an g-clár
Beiḋ suiliḋ geal', lonraċ' do d' ḟailtuġaḋ le geastail
 Agus giollaċt an ċumain air an ḃ-fleiḋ 'cur bárr.

II.

Is réir cosaṁail gur culuiġ ríġ an t-saoġail so ó ṫeallaċ
 An te úd d'a ṫugas roinn ṁór de do ġnaoi
Gaḃfair tabartais is aille no táinte go ballaċ
 A soilsiuġaḋ a ċois-céim a siuḃal anns an t-sliġe.

III.

Le saoirse na h-intine naċ feidir a ċasaḋ
 Le táir-ceannas treun biṫ, ó dire'as na sliġe
Bíḋeas gan cuiḃriġ air eitioll, 'gus aigne faoi lasaḋ
 Le dóiġ 'g ionsuiḋe 'n loċrain a santuiġ a ċroiḋe.

IV.

Is so iad a ḃeireas d' a ḃeaṫa a ḋilse
 Agus leis, ciḋ go ḃ-fuil a ċiste ro-gann
Bíḋeann saor-gaeṫe a ġarrḋa go mór-ṁór níos milse
 'Na an túr tearc m-bíḋeann uaḃar aig fáġail taiṫneaṁ ann.

V.

Tarraiḋ a's ma 's feidir le fleiḋ boċt an ḟile
 Do ṫarrangt ó ṁórdaċt, geaḃfair, ní se an dioġa,
Agus cluinféar na ḃinn-ċeoilte ḃearḟas duit bile
 Mo mná searc' aig singeaḋ aig teaċt le mo ṫaoḃ.

Nor frown was seen through sky or sea,
  Nor tear o'er leaf or sod,
When first on their Isle of Destiny
  Our great forefathers trod.

THOUGH HUMBLE THE BANQUET.

Air—*Farewell, Eamon.*

I.

Though humble the banquet to which I invite thee,
  Thou 'lt find there the best a poor bard can command:
Eyes beaming with welcome shall throng round to light thee,
  And Love serve the feast with his own willing hand.

II.

And tho' Fortune may seem to have turn'd from the dwelling
  Of him thou regardest, her favouring ray,
Thou wilt find there a gift all her treasures excelling,
  Which, proudly he feels, hath ennobled his way.

III.

'T is that freedom of mind, which no vulgar dominion
  Can turn from the path a clear conscience approves;
Which, with hope in the heart and no chain on the pinion,
  Holds upward its course to the light which it loves.

IV.

'T is this makes the pride of his humble retreat,
  And, with this, tho' of all other treasures bereav'd,
The breeze of his garden to him is more sweet
  Than the costliest incense Pomp e'er receiv'd.

V.

Then, come: if a board so untempting hath power
  To win thee from grandeur, its best shall be thine;
And there 's one, long the light of the bard's happy bower,
  Who, smiling, will blend her bright welcome with mine

'S NAĊ Ḃ-FAĠMUID Ó ĊRUINNUĠAḊ' MAR SO CIÚTUĠAḊ LÁN

Fonn—Ní'l fios air.

I.

'S naċ ḃ-faġmuid ó ċruinnuġaḋ mar so ciútuġaḋ lán
Air son na m-bliaḋanta measg coigriġ' do ḃí
'S caraid aimsire na h-óige ó'r culuiġear le fán,
Mo ṫimċioll ċo suairc a's ḃí 'n uair sin a g-croiḋe.
Cid foillsiġeann ar malaiḋ lorg sneaċta na h-aoise
Mar na h-Alpa air a sineann dul síos dí an ġrian
A ġaeṫe: beiḋmuid cuduiġ' le óg-rós' na baoise
Trá sinn a ḃeiṫ lasta san ḃ-fleiḋ so le fíon.

II.

Naċ moṫuġaṁail na cuiṁniḋ tig orainn le linn,
Ar g-cairde 'nír feicsint, 'sa 'ḃeiṫ nír eisteaċt a n-guṫ!
'S gaċ brón, a's gaċ gairdeas ann a raiḃ aca roinn
A ċruinnuġaḋ mar tairiḃ an lae nae go tiúġ.
Mar leitréaċ' neaṁ-leirsgaċ' do léiġtear 'sa tráṫ
N-biḋeann na duilleog' air aġaiḋ' na lasraċ' teo
Is iomḋá moṫuġaḋ nár cruoṫnuiġeaḋ ḃeir téagar a's gráḋ
Fleaḋ teisgraċ mar so 'maċ go soilseaċ a's go beo.

III.

Mar so tráṫ duinn síneaḋ ar seolta go cuiṁneaċ
Cum árais ar n-óige tríḋ ṁuir buairṫa ar m-biṫ
Do ċiḋmuid aig breaċnuġaḋ tríd na tonta go saiṁneaċ
Mórán doiġṫe luing-ḃriste síos sínte 'nna luiḋe.
Aċt fós le linn dearcaḋ air deire na m-blaṫ.
Sgeiṫ sgéiṁ' áluinn' gairḋa tríḋ iomlan an ċuain
Biḋeann feaḋ gearr aimsire ar g-ceudfaiḋ' faoi sgáṫ
'S tig aoiḃnis na h-óige ṫríd aislin ar suain.

AND DOTH NOT A MEETING LIKE THIS.

AIR—*Unknown.*

I.

And doth not a meeting like this make amends
For all the long years I 've been wand'ring away—
To see thus around me my youth's early friends,
As smiling and kind as in that happy day?
Tho' haply o'er some of your brows, as o'er mine,
The snow-fall of life may be stealing—what then?
Like Alps in the sunset, thus lighted by wine,
We 'll wear the gay tint of youth's roses again.

II.

What soften'd remembrances come o'er the heart
In gazing on those we 've been lost to so long!
The sorrows, the joys, of which once they were part,
Still round them, like visions of yesterday, throng.
As letters some hand hath invisibly trac'd,
When held to the flame, will steal out on the sight,
So many a feeling, that long seem'd effac'd,
The warmth of a moment like this brings to light.

III.

And thus, as in memory's bark we shall glide
To visit the scenes of our boyhood anew,
Though oft' we may see, looking down on the tide,
The wreck of full many a hope shining through;
Yet still, as in fancy we point to the flow'rs,
That once made a garden of all the gay shore,
Deceiv'd for a moment, we 'll think them still ours,
And breathe the fresh air of life's morning once more

IV.

Tá an saoġal so ċo neaṁ-ḃuan 'san n-am ann ċo gearr
  Naċ ḃ-faġam' air ar g-cairde aċt lag-leur neaṁ-ġrinn,
'Gur 's iomḋa sgaiċ ruaircis do ċuitear air lár
  De ḋiṫḃáil croiḋe ceanaṁal' gar ḋuinn, le n-a roinn.
O! níor ṁór ar ṁuinnġin n-eis ċríoċnuġaḋ ar m-biṫ
  Ḃeiṫ seilḃ air aoiḃneas gan críoċ 'gus gan sgáil,
Ní'l aċt smig no breiṫ-láiṁe aig deiċḟriuġaḋ 'sa t-sliġe
  O n-a ċéile san t-saoġal so a n-dán dúinn le faġail.

V.

Aċt is aṁlaiḋ, is mó 'r ḃ-fáilte, 's ar m-beannaċt le linn
  Cuairt anaṁ an t-siompsa aig tógḃail ar g-croiḋe
Euluiġeas trá sgaram' a's tig trá bíḋeam' cruinn
  Mar na tear-cunlaiḋ 'g eitioll aig an geiṁraḋ cur faoi.
'Nois sul da n-ólam' tugaḋ seare cuman geall,
  'Cur ċart na cuaice 's a breiṫ láṁ 'air laṁ
Ċo luaṫ 's ionsóċas gáirdeas no duḃrón aon ḃall
  Go g-cruṫiḋ' leis iomlán an t-slaḃraiḋ le dáṁ.

TÉIĠ ṪRID AN DOṀAN 'GUS TÓIRIG GAĊ DAIL.

Fonn—Planesti O'Raġallaiġ.

I.

Téiġ ṫrid an doṁan 'gus tóiruġ gaċ dáil,—
'S ní ḃ-fuiġ ait ċo saor a's tá aig File le Fáġail;
Mar ḟuiseóg an aer do ṡeinneas go binn,
'S mar an ḟuiseóg a sgéiṫ ann gaċ áit a rinn,
Sruṫ ceoil do riṫeas go ciún síor ḃeo
'S naċ tromuiġeann a ḃarr go deo.
Tá dó-san an saoġal, mar áit comnuiḋe siġe
'M-bíḋeann siad a rinc le linn geallaiġe na h-oiḋċe
'S ma ṁiltear an ḃainseog air a leagaḋ a g-céim,
Ċum bainseoig' níos glaise, súd leo de léim.
Mar súd ma ṫig duḃaċan air síams' no sgiṫ
Ċum síams' eile teiḋeann 'sa t-sliġe.

IV.

So brief our existence, a glimpse, at the most,
Is all we can have of the few we hold dear;
And oft' even joy is unheeded and lost,
For want of some heart, that could echo it, near.
Ah! well may we hope, when this short life is gone,
To meet in some world of more permanent bliss.
For a smile, or a grasp of the hand, hast'ning on,
Is all we enjoy of each other in this.

V.

But come! the more rare such delight to the heart,
The more we should welcome and bless them the more:
They 're ours when we meet—they are lost when we part,
Like birds that bring summer, and fly when 't is o'er.
Thus circling the cup, hand in hand, ere we drink,
Let Sympathy pledge us, thro' pleasure, thro' pain,
That, fast as a feeling but touches one link,
Her magic shall send it direct thro' the chain

THE WANDERING BARD.

Air—*Planxty O'Reilly.*

I.

What life like that of the bard can be—
The wandering bard, who roams as free
As the mountain lark that o'er him sings,
And, like that lark, a music brings
Within him, where'er he comes or goes,—
A fount that for ever flows?
The world 's to him like some play-ground,
Where fairies dance their moonlight round;—
If dimm'd the turf where late they trod,
The elves but seek some greener sod:
So, when less bright his scene of glee,
To another away flies he!

II.

Cia d' éiroċaḋ de 'n deise is sgiaṁaṁla bláṫ
Gan file 'g a coiṁeud fíor úr faoi sgáṫ,
Le leus cros-ċuairt na geallaiġe, faġṫar féin Sgeul,
Na neiṫe a cailtear air talaṁ faoi neul.
Mar súd n-éis imṫeaċt do 'n maise o'n t-saoġal
Ann sinn an Ḃaird maireann dé fuiġioll
Ma's áil leat smigeaḋ ḃeiṫ taiṫneaṁail, sior,
Tabair do 'n te iad b-fuil aige go fíor
Cumas le béim de ḟleasg na siġe,
A g congḃail ga cugaḋ n-eis ar m-biṫ,
'G a g-crocaḋ go lonraċ a speuir na m-baird
Og-reulta sior-beo 'g ór-áird.

III.

Fáilte do 'n File ann gaċ baile d 'a m-biḋeann
Cid 's iomad áit ann a m-brostuiġeann a ċlaon
Le cicioll neaṁ-ċuiḃreaċ aig dul gan sgiṫ
'Nois a's arís; 'na deiġ sin, se a ġnaoi,
Tuirlint ain talaṁ ċum suairceas faġail
Aṁail a's ḃeirees an Fleiḋ so a's dáil;
Is cuma cia an fad tá an aisdir no an luas
Ní 'l agad aċt óg-suile a lasaḋ suas,
Leus coṁarṫa mar tá ann so go léir,
Agus tiocfaiḋ an file a nuas ó 'o speuir
Cia 'r biṫ ait ann a g-cluinfaiḋ cuireaḋ dó, gáir
Le gráḋ. no le suairceas,—Ḃéarfar air, fáir.

A RUIN CUIR ORT 'SA TRAṪ.

Fonn—Cuma liom.

I.

A Rúin cuir ort 'sa tráṫ,
Na gaeṫe so soilseaċ' grianṁar'
'S ṫar an muir tá glas faoi ḃlaṫ
Béarfad ṫu go claonṁar,

II.

Oh! what would have been young Beauty's doom,
Without a bard to fix her bloom?
They tell us, in the moon's bright round,
Things lost in this dark world are found:
So charms, on earth long pass'd and gone,
In the poet's lay live on.—
Would ye have smiles that ne'er grow dim?
You've only to give them all to him,
Who, with but a touch of Fancy's wand,
Can lend them life, this life beyond,
And fix them high, in Poesy's sky,—
Young stars that never die!

III.

Then, welcome the bard where'er he comes;
For, though he hath countless airy homes,
To which his wing excursive roves,
Yet still, from time to time, he loves
To light upon earth, and find such cheer
As brightens our banquet here.
No matter how far, how fleet he flies,
You 've only to light up kind young eyes,
Such signal-fires as here are given,—
And down he 'll drop from Fancy's heaven,
The minute such call to love or mirth
Proclaims he 's wanting on earth!

FAIREST! PUT ON AWHILE.

Air—*Cuma liom.*

I.

Fairest! put on awhile
These pinions of light I bring thee,
And o'er thy own Green Isle
In fancy let me wing thee.

Sgiaṫa Aprel go fós a riaṁ
  Lár sgáil luiḋe-lac níor síneaḋ'
Air ċriċ ċo ḋear air gaċ taoḃ
  'S le aitios do ċroiḋe 'g a líonaḋ.

II.

Maġa 'm-biḋean earraċ go deo
  'Fuireaċt go deo neaṁ-sgaṫṁar
Le gaete na greine teo
  Gan sgiaṫ aċt a ḋeora blaṫṁar'
Mearg craoḃa muirṫil árd-ċraig'
  Go teann 's go bagraċ suiḋte
Mar ṁalaiḋ laoiċ neaṁ-lag
  Raiḃ orra craoḃ gráḋ' sigte.

III.

Innse ċo h-úr gan sgiṫ
  Naċ raiḃ eun a riaṁ naċ seasfaḋ
Aig eitioll dó 'sa t-slige
  'Cum cuairt airṫa, 'nuar naċ g-casfaḋ
Sud samail a óig an deaġ-deilḃ
  Ḃ-fuil ċo meurṫa a n-dearcaḋ
Go d-tuirliġeann gean neiṁe ságail seilḃ
  Air sgoide mearg mna, ċo tearca.

IV.

Loċa a m-biḋeann neaṁnaid 'sa linn
  'S cláirse le sgoide líonṁar,
Co geal leis na deora crinn
  Do ṫig ó do súiliḃ gruanṁar'.
'S gleanta a ḃ-faġann annta suan
  An ṁuir ó ḃruiṫ ḃorḃ-gaoiṫe
'S callaiḋ beir fargad buan
  Do 'Scólṫaiḃ saor' Eireann coiḋċe.

V.

Cosad a's beiḋeas—'s a ḃ-fuil dear a's mór
  Le aitios do ċroiḋe 'g a líonad'
Ma ḃiḋeann ċum uaill' go leor
  As do ṫír féin gráḋaċ aig claonaḋ

Never did Ariel's plume
  At golden sunset hover
O'er scenes so full of bloom
  As I shall waft thee over.

II.

Fields, where the Spring delays,
  And fearlessly meets the ardour
Of the warm Summer's gaze,
  With only her tears to guard her.
Rocks, through myrtle boughs
  In grace majestic frowning;
Like some bold warrior's brows
  That Love hath just been crowning.

III.

Islets, so freshly fair,
  That never hath bird come nigh them,
But from his course through air
  He hath been won down by them;
Types, sweet maid, of thee,
  Whose look, whose blush inviting,
Never did Love yet see
  From Heav'n, without alighting.

IV.

Lakes, where the pearl lies hid,
  And caves, where the gem is sleeping,
Bright as the tears thy lid
  Lets fall in lonely weeping.
Gems, where Ocean comes
  To 'scape the wild winds' rancour,
And Harbours, worthiest homes
  Where Freedom's fleet can anchor.

V.

Then, if, while scenes so grand,
  So beautiful, shine before thee,
Pride for thy own dear land
  Should haply be stealing o'er thee,

O! bídeað, ar túr, geur-ċaoið'
Os cionn uabair go brónmar
Gur mill lám fear an ċríċ
'Cum Dia na n-dúl ċo glórmar.

AIR MAIDIN AR M-BEAṪA.

Fonn—Nór beag an Foġmair.

I.

Air maidin ar m-beaṫa 's a brón for faoi sgáṫ
'S an riamra 'g a foillsiuġað go h-úr air ar sliġe
'Nuair is linn féin an saoġal atá iomlán faoi bláṫ
'Sa leur tá 'n-ar d-timcioll tig sgeite ó 'n g-croiðe.
Ní gnasamail! feað, creid me 'san am úd do 'n grád,
Beiṫ ruaġalta mar 's dual faoi ċuing céile 'gur aoir
Do ruigeað 's do muinigin breaġ grianmar, re an tráṫ,
Aċt is teagaraiġe an cuman n-éir coluġað do 'n m-baoir

II.

'Nuair imeiġear gan filleað sgaiṫ ar n-oige go deo
Mar duilleog 'g a seolað le fána 'sa t-sruṫ
'Nuair bleras ar sgála le riamr' lonrað beo
Braon de'n cuaċ eile tá síor searb, dub.
Súd, Súd, an t-am a m-bídeann searc-cuman croiðe
Foillsiuġað dilse naċ d-tigeann riamra go h-eug
Grád beirtear as buaireað, mar an m-buaireað sior bíð
'N grád a oiltear le tlaċt, ní'l mar tlaċt ann,—aċt breug.

III.

A g-créiḃ geal' griaṁar' gið is aoibin a m-bláṫ
Is lag é an balað ó n-a gogain, a's fann
Sí an sgeur féin tá ceaṫaċ faoi neulta a's faoi sgaṫ
Beir 'maċ a imlseaċt go h-ionlán neaṁ-ġann.
A'S sunda, feað lastar na h-anċlaonta teo
Aċt a mbrón, feað a feicctear an cuman tá sior
Cið as ruigið é foillsiuġað air d-túr ṫarla dó
As deora tarrangtar a imlseaċt go síor.

Oh! let grief come first,
  O'er pride itself victorious,
Thinking how man hath curst
  What Heaven had made so glorious!

IN THE MORNING OF LIFE.

AIR—*The Little Harvest Rose.*

I

In the morning of life, when its cares are unknown,
  And its pleasures in all their new lustre begin,
When we live in a bright-beaming world of our own,
  And the light that surrounds us is all from within;
Oh! 't is not, believe me, in that happy time
  We can love, as in hours of less transport we may:—
Of our smiles, of our hopes, 't is the gay sunny prime,
  But affection is truest when these fade away.

II.

When we see the first glory of youth pass us by,
  Like a leaf on the stream that will never return;
When our cup, which had sparkled with pleasure so high,
  First tastes of the *other*, the dark-flowing urn;
Then, then is the time when affection holds sway
  With a depth and a tenderness joy never knew;
Love nurs'd among pleasures, is faithless as they,
  But the love born of Sorrow, like Sorrow, is true.

III.

In climes full of sunshine, though splendid the flowers,
  The sighs have no freshness, their odour no worth;
'T is the cloud and the mist of our own Isle of showers
  That call the rich spirit of fragrancy forth.
So it is not 'mid splendour, prosperity, mirth,
  That the depth of Love's generous spirit appears;
To the sunshine of smiles it may first owe its birth,
  But the soul of its sweetness is drawn out by tears.

TRÁṪ EIRE ḂEIṪ.

Fonn—Uisge na Boinne.

I.

Tráṫ Eire ḃeiṫ air ḃruaċ an Linn'
  Na Boinne an ṁ-áḋ' cráiḋte
Dearc 'n áit ar ṫeilg an t-Strig 's an toinn
  An Tairg' a raiḃ gaeṫe ann saiṫte,
"A ġaeṫe ṁiṁaṁail," árd do ḃlaoiġ,
  "Fanaiḋ ann sin faoi ḟolaċ"
"Oir tá siḃ smearṫa le fuil croiḋe"
  "'Ḋoirt gairgiḋ' dam go ballaċ."

II.

Aċt tá 'gul 's a guiḋċ gan aon ḃriġ,
  Mar soillsiġear bailte bána;
An Andrear 'ḃliantaṁail tig gan sgiṫ
  Agus teiḋeann 'sa t-sruṫ le fána:
'Gur ḃeir as gaeṫe ṁiṁaṁail teo,
  'G a sgaoleaḋ go teann treunṁar
Measg daoine a tá buile-ḃeo
  'Ga g-congḃail go sior, leunṁar

III.

Mo nuair! go Eirinn na súl táir'
  Air ḃruaċ na Boinne sínte;
Tigeann aindrear gan aon tuirse air ais,
  'S a tairg' le gaeṫe lionta.
O Ḋia! 'm-béiḋ tiarna! le trom ġuṫ
  Air m' ansoġ,—lá 'gur oiḋċe
Sgreadann, a's freagrar Deaṁon ó 'n t-sruṫ,
  "Ni ḃeiḋ, ni ḃéiḋ, a ċoiḋċe."

AS VANQUISH'D ERIN.

Air—*The Boyne Water.*

I.

As vanquish'd Erin wept beside
  The Boyne's ill-fated river,
She saw where Discord, in the tide,
  Had dropp'd his loaded quiver.
"Lie hid", she cried, "ye venom'd darts,
  "Where mortal eye may shun you.
"Lie hid: the stain of manly hearts
  "That bled for me, is on you".

II.

But vain her wish, her weeping vain—
  As Time too well hath taught her—
Each year the Fiend returns again,
  And dives into that water;
And brings, triumphant, from beneath
  His shafts of desolation,
And sends them, wing'd with worse than death,
  Through all her madd'ning nation.

III.

Alas for her who sits and mourns,
  Ev'n now, beside that river!—
Unwearied still the Fiend returns,
  And stor'd is still his quiver.
"When will this end, ye Powers of Good?'
  She weeping asks for ever:
But only hears, from out that flood,
  The Demon answer, "Never!"

Ḃeiṫ Siuḃal tri Cruinneaḋ lán de Ċraḋ.

Fonn—Siúbail a Rúin.

I.

Ḃeiṫ siuḃal tri ċruinneaḋ lán de ċráḋ
'S de ċuma faoi gur d' eulaiġ an blaṫ
Sgar súile meangaċ' 's ceolta binn
Air fúd an ċosáin le n-ar linn
Súd, Súd, an iod go deo
Ḃeiḋear air gaċ neaċ d' a ḃ-fanfaiḋ ḃeo
'N-éis eug na g-caraḋ ċuaiḋ faoi śuan
'S a sileaḋ, 'd-fanfaḋ linn go buan.

II.

Ciḋ ta dream óga 'fás gaċ lá
Ní dúinn tá a smigeaḋ 'n-dán sa tráṫ,
Tá 'teastail uaṫa an lóċran síġe,
Naċ ḃ-faġṫar aċt le gean an ċroiḋe.
Ca ḃ-fuil, ca ḃ-fuil an ṁallaiḋ ṁín
No an comraḋ ceannaṁail, ceolṁar, caoin,
Ciḋ táim 'ga d-tóruiġeaċt ann gaċ dáil,
A lorg, ni'l faraoir! le fáġail.

III.

Tá stuam luċt cumṫa gan aon ḃríġ
Mar d-tig leis dúsaċt ann's an g-croiḋe
Gaċ tláiṫ ṫug dúinn súile beo
Tá faraoir! baiṫte 'nois faoi ċeo.
Ní fusa croiḋe an te tá crom
Faoi uallaċ aoise a's buaireaḋ trom,
Le téagair siams' arís a ṫeiġeaḋ
No, a ṫabairt air ais ó leaba créaḋ

ALONE IN CROWDS TO WANDER ON.

Air—*Siubhal A Rúin.*

I.

Alone in crowds to wander on,
And feel that all the charm is gone
Which voices dear and eyes belov'd
Shed round us once, where'er we rov'd—
This, this the doom must be
Of all who 've lov'd, and liv'd to see
The few bright things they thought would stay
For ever near them, fly away.

II.

Tho' fairer forms around us throng,
Their smiles to others all belong,
And want that charm which dwells alone
Round those the fond heart calls its own.
Where, where the sunny brow?
The long-known voice—where are they now?
Thus ask I still, nor ask in vain,
The silence answers all too plain.

III.

Oh! what is Fancy's magic worth,
If all her art cannot call forth
One bliss like those we felt of old
From lips now mute, and eyes now cold?
No, no,—her spell is vain,—
As soon could she bring back again
Those eyes themselves from out the grave,
As wake again one bliss they gave.

IS TRUAĠ GAN ME A Ḃ-FOĊAR SRUṪ'.

Fonn—B'ḟeárr liom go m-beiḋinn air an g-cnoc úd ṫall.

I.

Is truaġ gan me a ḃ-foċar sruṫ'
Na loċa ciúinṁar' ḃrónaċ' duḃ',
Ann a d-teiḋeann aiṫriġiġ ó 'n t-saoġal roiṁ rac
Ann eidiġ' báis, sul dul faoi 'n g-cré:
Ann sin do ġeaḃfainn didion 's cuan
'S a ḃ-fad ó 'n t-saoġal tá meallṫaċ,—suan;
Ni ġoillfeaḋ pian;—air ṡaiṁs' 's a ċeilg
Ni ċuirfinn feard' a ċoiḋċe seilg.

II.

An t-aer mar ċill gan leaċta ḃiṫ,
Fuaim trom na sruṫ' naċ ḃ-feicṫear faoi;
Na dilleog' crion' ó ḃárr na g-crann,
Mor ṫaiḃriḋ luasgan ṫar do ċeann;
So ṡiad, so ṡiad ḃeir do 'n ċroiḋe
Fios air ċluan an t-saoġail 's 'neaṁ-ḃriġ,
'Gur mar na silleog' le cinn crom'
Ḃeir buill 'na uaiġe smuainte trom'

III.

An ċoineall soilseaċ duinn do las,
Cum codlaḋ ḟáġail do cuirtear as,
Mar súd gaċ doiġe do sgrias an croiḋe
Cum suaiṁnis sealḃuġaḋ is dual do ċlaoiḋ.
Is fuar, fuar mo ċroiḋe do ḃeiḋeas
Gan aṫruġaḋ ó ḋuḃaċan no ó leus
Mar tobar sastuiġṫe a slaḃraiḋ seac
Iompuiġṫear a d-tleigṫear ann, 'nna leac

I WISH I WAS BY THAT DIM LAKE.

Air—*I wish I was on yonder hill.*

I.

I wish I was by that dim lake
Where sinful souls their farewell take
Of this vain world, and half-way lie
In death's cold shadow, ere they die.
There, there, far from thee,
Deceitful world, my home should be;
Where, come what might of gloom and pain,
False hope should ne'er deceive again.

II.

The lifeless sky, the mournful sound
Of unseen waters falling round,
The dry leaves quiv'ring o'er my head,
Like man, unquiet ev'n when dead!
These, ay, these shall wean
My soul from life's deluding scene,
And turn each thought, o'ercharg'd with gloom,
Like willows downward tow'rds the tomb.

III.

As they who to their couch at night
Would win repose, first quench the light,
So must the hopes that keep this breast
Awake, be quench'd, ere it can rest.
Cold, cold this heart must grow,
Unmov'd by either joy or wo,
Like freezing founts, where all that 's thrown
Within their current turns to stone.

ABRAN ROIṀ LAE AN ĊOGAIḊ.

Fonn—Crúiscín Lán.

I.

Co cinte ar támuid leo
Béiḋmuid 'maraċ anns an gleo,
  Le ḃeiṫ buaḋaċ, no anns an ár 'n-ar luiḋe:
Tá an ṁaidin fáinuġaḋ bán
'Gus le fíon ar sgála lán,
  'S ólam' deoċ, roiṁ dúinn triall anns an t-sliġe, anns an t-sliġe,
  'S ólam' deoċ roiṁ dúinn triall anns an t-sliġe.

II.

Trí súiliḃ misniġ móir,
Briseann 'maċ go minic deor,
  Meaṁruġaḋ ar g-cáirde fágaḋ aonraċ a g-cúl
Aċt naċ diṁaoin ḃeiṫ silt braon
Co'ad tá sgála sgairdaḋ fíon'
  'S le n-a ḋeoraiḃ dibream' uainn deor ar súl, deor ar súl, etc.

III.

Tá solus geal an lae,—
An la deiġionaċ 'sear a ġae
  Air ar leinḃ a rinne ar d-timpioll le roġ:
A máraċ roiṁ an oiḋċe
Ca m-béiḋmuid 's iad n-ar luiḋe?
  Aċt naċ cuma!—fastuiġiḋ an lann ċum an gleo;—ċum an gleó, etc.

IV.

Fanaḋ an meud ta feaċta, faon
Faoi ċuing Sacsan a's Loċlan deann
  Faireaḋ gríosaiġ an teallaiġ san tráṫ
Aon urna air son ar d-tiġ
'S go neaṁ suas orṫa ó ċroiḋe
  'S air son Eireann' gus a clainn' hurra! hurra! hurra!
  'S air son Eireann 'gus a clainn' hurra!

SONG OF THE BATTLE EVE.

TIME, THE NINTH CENTURY.

Air—Cruiskin Lan.

I.

To-morrow, comrade, we
On the battle-plain must be,
  There to conquer, or both lie low!
The morning-star is up,—
But there 's wine still in the cup,
  And we 'll take another quaff ere we go, boy, go:
  We 'll take another quaff ere we go.

II.

'Tis true, in manliest eyes
A passing tear will rise,
  When we think of the friends we leave lone;
But what can wailing do?
See, our goblet 's weeping too!
  With its tears we 'll chase away our own, boy, our own;
  With its tears we 'll chase away our own.

III.

But daylight 's stealing on;—
The last that o'er us shone
  Saw our children around us play:
The next—ah! where shall we
And those rosy urchins be?
  But—no matter--grasp thy sword, and away, boy, away;
  No matter--grasp thy sword, and away!

IV.

Let those, who brook the chain
Of Saxon or of Dane,
  Ignobly by their firesides stay;
One sigh to home be given,
One heartfelt prayer to heaven,
  Then for Erin and her cause, boy, hurra! hurra! hurra!
  Then for Erin and her cause, hurra!

Leag an Lann le n-a ṫaoḃ.

Fonn—Da ḃuḋ dubaċ an ṁuir lán.

I.

Leag an lann le n-a ṫaoḃ,—raiḃ a ċoimgioll ro ḟíor
  Gan a ċur leis 'san g-cré ann a ḃ-fuil faoi ṫaṁ
Cneasta ann gaċ am, sul d'ar ṫuit ó'n láṁ saor
  Bí 'ḃárr iompuiġṫe 's é air teiṫeaḋ fós 'n-aġaiḋ an naṁ.
Co-oiḃriġṫe le n-a m-beo, teiḋeaḋ ċum suain taoḃ le taoḃ,
  Mar is cuiḃe do ḋís treunṁar' dul ċum sgiṫ,
An lann iomlán ann a sgáṫ 'raiḃ gean aige a riaṁ
  'S é féin buaḋaċ 'san uaiġ 'nna luiḋe.

II.

Aċt éist; óir, a sílim beiṫ aig eisteaċt le guṫ
  Teaċt a níos ó 'n g-croiḋe treun a ḃí dáiṁaṁail le buaiḋ
Fann freagairt air an geur-gráig do ḃris mar ṫeann-sruṫ
  Air ċluais daoine aig fuagraḋ, " ḃris ḃur slaḃraiḋ cruaiḋe":
Agus gáireann as an uaiġ ann a g-codlann an luan,
  Cid tá lá air d-toisiġ go síor faoi ċeo,
O! na fagaiḋ a lann, neaṁ ġlóirṁar faoi ṡuan
  'S ċum buaiḋe tá fós ann, deo.

III.

Da ngaḃfaḋ ann féin aon ċoigcriġeaċ gan céim a's gan clú
  Buaint leat, mo lann féin, sínte ann do sgaṫ
Mar cloiḋeaṁ draoiḋeaċta faoi ṡeula go dluṫ,
  No fill go h-uaiġ do ṫiġearna gan céim le n-a ċráḋ.
Aċt ma ḟastuiġeann aon láṁ treun-ġaisgiġ saoir
  Ċleaċt lann geal mar ṫu imirt 'san g-caṫ le céim,
Le blaoiḋ saoirse ligṫe go luaṫ mar an ċaor
  As d' ṫruaill bí amuiġ air de léim.

LAY HIS SWORD BY HIS SIDE.

Air—*If the sea were ink.*

I.

Lay his sword by his side, it hath serv'd him too well
Not to rest near his pillow below;
To the last moment true, from his hand ere it fell,
Its point was still turn'd to a flying foe.
Fellow-lab'rers in life, let them slumber in death,
Side by side, as becomes the reposing brave,
That sword which he lov'd still unbroken in its sheath,
And himself unsubdued in his grave.

II.

Yet pause! for, in fancy, a still voice I hear,
As if breath'd from his brave heart's remains;—
Faint echo of that which, in Slavery's ear,
Once sounded the war-word, "Burst your chains!"
And it cries, from the grave where the hero lies deep:
"Tho' the day of your Chieftain for ever hath set,
"Oh! leave not his sword thus inglorious to sleep,—
"It hath victory's life in it yet!

III.

"Should some alien, unworthy such weapon to wield,
"Dare to touch thee, my own gallant sword,
"Then rest in thy sheath, like a talisman seal'd,
"Or return to the grave of thy chainless lord.
"But if grasp'd by a hand that hath learn'd the proud use
"Of a falchion, like thee, on the battle-plain,—
"Then, at Liberty's summons, like lightning let loose,
"Leap forth from thy dark sheath again".

O ÁRAIN ṀÓIR!

Fonn—Aonaċ Cille Ḋrongaill.

I.

O Árain ṁóir! ċaoiṁ! Árain ṁóir!
Is ionḋual ann's an oiḋċe,
Do ṡmuainim ort trá ḃí me óg
'Gur luaiṫneaċ mar an ġaoṫ.
Ciḋ ṡiuḃal me bealláiġ cam' an t-saoġail
Aig toiṙeaċt féin a's suain
Ní ḃ-fuair me an soġ buḋ cleaċtaċ liom
Go h-uaigneaċ air do ċuan.

II.

Buḋ ṁoċ air ḃruaċ na h-aille me,
Aig fánuġaḋ an lae le fonn;
'S mo ċroiḋe ċo leimneaċ leis na m-bain
Ḃí rinnc air ḃárr na d-tonn:
No, 'nuair a lasuiġeaḋ an ṁuir ḋuḃ
Le ór-sgáil lae aig dul faoi
Do ċóiriġeas Parṫas ann's a' t-sruṫ,
A lár an lóċrain ḃuiḋe.

III.

An Parṫas 'a g-coṁnuiġeann sgaiṫ na ḃ-Fian
'D-Tír álainn úr gan eug,
A ċiḋtear aig dul luiḋe do 'n ġréin
Mar sgeuluiġeas filiḋeaċt ḃreug.
'Ḃ-fuil fírin' ann,—sna " tiġṫe 'toinn",
Tá aig éaluġaḋ uainn gan sgiṫ,
'Siad saṁail aisling óig' neaṁ-ġrinn'
Co ġrianṁar 's fós gan bríġ.

O ARANMORE, LOV'D ARANMORE!

AIR—*Killdronghall Fair.*

I.

O Aranmore, lov'd Aranmore!
  How oft' I dream of thee,
And of those days when, by thy shore,
  I wander'd young aud free!
Full many a path I 've tried since then,
  Through pleasure's flowery maze,
But ne'er could find the bliss again
  I felt in those sweet days.

II.

How blithe upon thy breezy cliffs
  At sunny morn I 've stood,
With heart as bounding as the skiffs
  That danc'd along thy flood;
Or, when the western wave grew bright
  With daylight's parting wing
Have sought that Eden in the ight
  Which dreaming poets sing;

III.

That Eden where th' immortal brave
  Dwell in a land serene,—
Whose bow'rs beyond the shining wave
  At sunset, oft' are seen.
Ah dream too full of sadd'ning truth!
  Those mansions o'er the main
Are like the hopes I built in youth,—
  As sunny and as vain!

SEINN A ĊAOIṀ ĊRUIT!

Fonn—Ní'l fios air.

I.

Seinn a ċaoiṁ-ċruit, dam-sa féinn
  Ceol air an am a bí,
A dúsóċas le n-a gaeṫe binn'
  Brón cuiṁne ann ar g-croiḋe:
Ceol a ṁeaṁróċas dúinn árd-tuaḋ
  Sgeiṫ solus air ar slíġe,
'Gus gaisgiḋ ṁór' le baird 'g luaḋ
  'S doiġe 'nois, faoi ṡmúid na h-oiḋċe.
Seinn a ċruit ċaoiṁ, dam-sa féinn,
  Is ionnan ar g-cran go deo,
Do 'n t-saoġal so, feard' ní ḃaineann sinn
  A g-cian aṁáin táim' beo.

II.

Naċ brónaċ osnaiġeal gaeṫ' na h-oiḋċe
  Measg do ṫeuda fann!
Aṁail stáirḋeaċt tuairisg guṫ na ríġ
  Nar cluineaḋ le fad' ann:
Guṫ cinnfeart 'tá 'nois faoi gáil,
  Raiḃ a d-tuaṫ, reir mear' síor-ḃuan
'Guis fíliḋ sealḃaḋ céim' a's cáil'
  Gan ainm 'nois faoi suan.
A ċruit 'tá osnaiġil guṫ na h-oiḋċe.
  Measg do ṫeud' fann
Is díṁaoin tuairisc guṫ na ríġ
  Le fada naċ raiḃ ann.

SING, SWEET HARP.

AIR—*Unknown.*

I.

Sing, sweet Harp, oh! sing to me
  Some song of early days,
Whose sounds, in this sad memory
  Long buried dreams shall raise:—
Some ray that tells of vanish'd flame,
  Whose light once round us shone:
Of noble pride, now turn'd to shame,
  And hopes for ever gone.
Sing, sad Harp, thus sing to me;
  Alike our doom is cast,
Both lost to all but memory,
  We live but in the past.

II.

How mournfully the midnight air
  Among thy chords doth sigh,
As if it sought some echo there
  Of voices long gone by:
Of chieftains, now forgot, who seem'd
  The foremost then in fame;
Of bards who, once immortal deem'd,
  Now sleep without a name.
In vain, sad Harp, the midnight air
  Among thy chords doth sigh
In vain it seeks an echo there
  Of voices long gone by.

III.

Dár b' ḟeidir duit-se blaoċ air ais
  Cum na boṫan geug
Na gaisgiḋ' d 'éist leat, anois 'nna d-táis'
  A's sostaċ 'neis dóiḃ eug
Cad fáċ, ní éiroċaiḋ cúiṁ' le deor,
  Beiċ cuiṁnuġaḋ brúid' clan daor.
Fag iad, mar sin, faoi ċaiṁ go leor,
  Tá na mai, b aṁain saor.
Sost, a ċruit ċrom ceuil na h-uaiṁ'
  Fuaim fuagraḋ luiḋe lae.
Na soirse no 'g éisteaċt leat le cúiṁ',
  Teiḋċam, seasda' sios faoi 'n g-cré.

III.

Couldst thou but call those spirits round,
  Who once, in bower and hall,
Sat listening to thy magic sound,
  Now mute and mould'ring all;—
But, no; they would but wake to weep
  Their children's slavery;
Then leave them in their dreamless sleep,
  The dead at least are free!—
Hush, hush, sad Harp, that dreary tone,
  That knell of Freedom's day;
Or, list'ning to its death-like moan,
  Let me, too, die away.

APPENDIX.

An Deoraiḋ as Éirinn.

I.

Ṫainic ċum na tráiġ' an deoraiḋ as Éirinn
Ḃuḋ trom, fuar an drúċt air' fálain ḃí san,
Ḃí aig osnaġail faoi n-a ṫír féin trá roiṁ eiriġ na gréine,
Ṡiúḃail le ais an ċnoic 'ḃuail an ṁuir, ḃorḃ teann.
Ḋearc se air reult na maidne go sár grinn
A d'éiriġ air a inis féin ḃí falcuiġṫe leis an lán toinn
Ann ar gnaṫaċ do ḃeiṫ seinim go croiḋaṁail 's go h-árd-binn
An t-aḃran ḃreáġ tíraṁail, "Eire go bráṫ".

II.

"Is truaġ e mo ḃeaṫa" ar 'n deoraiḋ boċt, craiḋte,
"Faġann an fiaċ agus an faol-ċú fasgaḋ ann gaċ gleann
Aċt agam-sa ní'l dídean o'n leun 'nna ḃ-fuilim báite
Ḃaile, no áit coṁnuiġe, ní ḃ-fuil agam ann;
Ni liom ḃeiṫ arís anns a g-craoḃ-ḃoṫan trílseaċ
Ann ar ċaiṫ mo ċeap-sinsir a n-aimsir go dílseaċ
No le bláḋ' aig gleus mo ċlarsaiġ ċum aḃrann ḃreaġ, milseaċ
Do ṫarrangt as a ṫeudaiḃ binn', "Eire go bráṫ".

APPENDIX.

THE EXILE OF ERIN.

I.

There came to the beach a poor exile of Erin;
The dew on his thin robe was heavy and chill;
For his country he sigh'd when at twilight repairing
To wander alone by the wind-beaten hill;
But the day-star attracted his eye's sad devotion,
For it rose o'er his own native isle of the ocean,
Where once in the fire of his youthful emotion
He sang the bold anthem of Erin-go-Brath.

II.

Oh! sad is my fate, said the heart-broken stranger:
The wild deer and wolf to a covert can flee;
But I have no refuge from famine and danger,
A home and a country remain not to me.
Ah! never again in the green sunny bowers
Where my forefathers lived, shall I spend the sweet hours,
Or cover my harp with the wild-woven flowers,
And strike to the numbers of Erin-go-Brath.

III.

Éire! mo ṫír féin, cí fagṫa go leunṁar
Ann mo aisling' ḃeirim cuairt air do ċuanta breaġ, gráḋaċ,
Aċt faraoir! a d-tír coigcreaċ, dúsġaim neaṁ-ċlaonṁar
Aig osnaġail fa mo ġaoltaiḃ naċ ċirid go bráṫ:
O mo ċruaḋ ċinaṁuin ḃ-fuil se a n-dán dam
'Ḃeiṫ 'sealḃ árais sioċċain' gan leanan baoġail go gnaṫaċ liom?
De mo ḃraṫairiḃ 's mo ċadairc ni ḃeiḋ aon go bráṫ liom
Fuair bás le mo ċomairc no mo ċaoineaḋ d' ḟan beo.

IV.

Ca ḃ-fuil ionsuiḋe mo ḃoṫain, ḃ-focair na coille craoḃaiġe?
Ḋeirḟiúra 'gur áṫair ar ċaoin siḃ iad air lár?
Ca ḃ-fuil an ṁaṫair ḃí aig áirdail m' óg laeṫe?
No ca ḃ-fuil mo ċairde d' ṫug a 'gean orṫa uil' bárr?
O mo ċroiḋe ḃrónaċ a ḃ-fad fagṫa go leanṁar
'S mairg a ḃí teann ar an neaṁ-ḃuan seunṁar!
'S fras do ṫig na deora uainn buarṫa 'gur aonṁar
Aċt fuaras 'gur deire, ni tiocfaiḋ air ais go bráṫ.

V.

Aċt 'néis gaċ' gráḋaċ cuiṁne a ċosg réir mo ċuṁaċta
Tiocfaiḋ aon ais-rún aṁáin ó mo ċroiḋe;
Eire ḃeir deoraiḋ a ḃeannaċt duit le uaċta,
Tír mo ċeap-sinsir! Eire a ċoiḋċe!
Trá ḃeiḋċas me sínte ann uaiṁ ḟuar na cille
Glas biḋeaḋ do ṁaġa, "1" ḃreaġ na tuile
'Gur le díoġras seuabfad clársaċ 'seinfaiḋ an file
Eire mo ṁuirnín! Eire go bráṫ!

III.

Erin, my country, though sad and forsaken,
 In dreams I revisit thy sea-beaten shore ;
But, alas ! in a far, foreign land I awaken,
 And sigh for the friends who can meet me no more.
O cruel fate, wilt thou never replace me
In a mansion of peace, where no perils can chase me ?
Ah ! never again shall my brothers embrace me,
 They died to defend me, or live to deplore.

IV.

Where is my cabin-door, fast by the wild-wood?
 Sisters and sire, did you weep for its fall ?
Where is the mother that looked on my childhood ?
 And where is the bosom friend dearer than all ?
O my sad heart ! long abandoned by pleasure,
Why did it dote on a fast-fading treasure ?
Tears, like the rain-drop, may fall without measure,
 But rapture and beauty they cannot recall.

V.

Yet, all its sad recollections suppressing,
 One dying wish my lone bosom can draw—
Erin, an exile bequeaths thee his blessing,
 Land of me forefathers—Erin-go-Brath !
Buried and cold, when my heart stills its motion,
Green be thy fields, sweetest isle of the ocean,
And thy harp-striking bards sing aloud with devotion,
 Erin mavourneen, Erin-go-Brath !

To the courtesy of the Messrs. LONGMAN, GREEN, AND Co., London, the reader is indebted for the rare advantage of having in the present edition of the MELODIES, the English original of the later songs of Moore with the Irish Version placed before him in juxtaposition.

To the application made to them on the subject, they write: "We have no objection to the Archbishop of Tuam publishing the English words of 'Moore's Irish Melodies', along with his translation in the Irish language".

www.ingramcontent.com/pod-product-compliance
Lightning Source LLC
Chambersburg PA
CBHW031439160426
43195CB00010BB/790
* 9 7 8 3 7 4 4 7 1 3 0 5 4 *